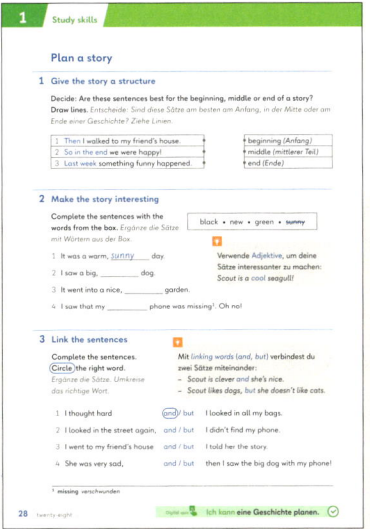

Study skills

Hier übst du wichtige Lerntechniken.

Unit task

In der *Unit task* erstellst du ein größeres Produkt, z.B. eine Präsentation.

Checkpoint

Hier überprüfst du, wie gut du gelernt hast.

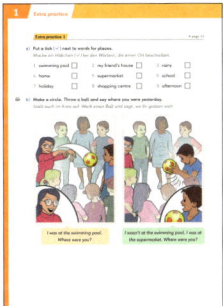

Extra practice

Am Ende jeder Unit findest du noch mehr Übungen.

Vokabelliste

Am Ende jeder Unit gibt es eine Liste mit den neuen Vokabeln. Blaue Wörter kennst du aus der Grundschule.

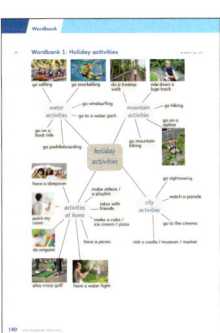

Wordbanks

Du hast neue Themen kennengelernt. Nach den Units findest du weitere Wörter dazu.

lighthouse 2

Lern- und Arbeitsheft für Lernende mit erhöhtem Förderbedarf

Im Auftrag des Verlages herausgegeben von
Martin Bastkowski, Schellerten; Sonja Mahne, Basel;
Ulrike Rath, Aachen; Berit Schaarschmidt, Aschaffenburg

Erarbeitet von
Rebecca Robb Benne, Kopenhagen; Zoe Thorne, Royston
sowie Olivia Wintgens, Aachen;
Jennifer O'Hagan, Bristol (*Checkpoints*)

In Zusammenarbeit mit der Englischredaktion
Klaus Unger (Projektleitung), Sandhya Gupta, Karin Wedepohl,
sowie Georg Raspe, Düsseldorf (*Vocabulary*)

Beratende Mitwirkung
Stella Halank, Berlin; Lina Hein, Wuppertal;
Christina McCrum, Köln

Medienmanagement
Silke Kirchhoff

Illustrationen
Harald Ardeias, Schelklngen; Irina Zinner, Hamburg;
Josephine Bienert-Köhler, Berlin

Fotos
Anja Poehlmann, Brighton
Für die freundliche Unterstützung danken wir der
Varndean School, Brighton

Umschlaggestaltung
Rosendahl, Berlin

Layoutkonzept
Klein & Halm, Berlin

Layout und technische Umsetzung
Straive

www.cornelsen.de

Soweit in diesem Lehrwerk Personen fotografisch abgebildet sind und ihnen von der Redaktion fiktive Namen, Berufe, Dialoge und Ähnliches zugeordnet oder diese Personen in bestimmte Kontexte gesetzt werden, dienen diese Zuordnungen und Darstellungen ausschließlich der Veranschaulichung und dem besseren Verständnis des Buchinhaltes.

Dieses Werk berücksichtigt die Regeln der reformierten Rechtschreibung und Zeichensetzung.

Die Webseiten Dritter, deren Internetadressen in diesem Lehrwerk angegeben sind, wurden vor Drucklegung sorgfältig geprüft. Der Verlag übernimmt keine Gewähr für die Aktualität und den Inhalt dieser Seiten oder solcher, die mit ihnen verlinkt sind.

Die **Cornelsen Lernen App** ist eine fakultative Ergänzung zu *Lighthouse*, die die inhaltliche Arbeit begleitet und unterstützt.

1. Auflage, 1. Druck 2023

Alle Drucke dieser Auflage sind inhaltlich unverändert und können im Unterricht nebeneinander verwendet werden.

ISBN 9783060358526 (Ausgabe für Lernende)
ISBN 9783060358540 (Ausgabe für Lehrkräfte)

Druck: H. Heenemann, Berlin

PEFC zertifiziert
Dieses Produkt stammt aus nachhaltig bewirtschafteten Wäldern und kontrollierten Quellen.
www.pefc.de

PEFC/04-31-1156

lighthouse 2

Lern- und Arbeitsheft

🔊🌐 **Audios** online verfügbar unter
www.cornelsen.de/webcodes　　**Code:** tateba

 Dein Arbeitsheft findest du auch in der **Cornelsen Lernen App**.

Siehst du eines dieser Symbole in deinem Arbeitsheft, findest du in der App …

🔊　alle **Audios**

▶️　alle **Videos** und **Erklärfilme**

　Hilfen und **Lösungen** zu ausgewählten Aufgaben

Cornelsen

Inhalt

Hello again!
The last day of the holidays

Wenn du die Seiten bearbeitet hast, setze ein Häkchen in die Box.

| Ready for school | **Ich kann verstehen, wie andere sich fühlen.**

I'm happy.
It's nice to see my friends again.
I'm not happy.
I want to have more free time. | | 10 ☐ |
| A day at Brighton beach | **Ich kann über Sommeraktivitäten sprechen.**

I'm looking at the sea.
Some people are swimming.
A boy is eating ice cream.
A girl is playing badminton. | | 11 ☐ |

Unit 1 Travel and holidays

Wenn du die Seiten bearbeitet hast, setze ein Häkchen in die Box.

Seite

Travel and holidays	**Ich kann über meine Ferien und das Wetter sprechen.** I was in Spain, in a hotel near the beach. The weather was hot and sunny.		12–13 ☐
Topic 1	**Ich kann über meine Ferienaktivitäten schreiben.** My family went to France by car. We had some pizza. I looked after my little sister.		14–17 ☐
Topic 2	**Ich kann über einen besonderen Tag in meinen Ferien sprechen.** Pride was so cool. I went with my friends. We had a great time!		18–21 ☐
Topic 3	**Ich kann über das letzte Wochenende sprechen.** Last weekend I played video games. I didn't make my bed.		22–23 ☐
Story	**Ich kann über neue Erfahrungen sprechen.** I travelled to my grandma's house alone for the first time.		24–26 ☐
Study skills	**Ich kann eine Geschichte planen.** A story has a beginning, a middle and an end.		28 ☐
Unit task	**Ich kann eine Geschichte erzählen.** Last summer I wanted a new bike, but I needed more money.		29 ☐

Unit 2 **Friends and heroes**

Wenn du die Seiten bearbeitet hast, setze ein Häkchen in die Box.

Unit 3 Activities and games

Wenn du die Seiten bearbeitet hast, setze ein Häkchen in die Box.

Unit 4 Celebrate!

Wenn du die Seiten bearbeitet hast, setze ein Häkchen in die Box.

Unit 4 Celebrate!

Unit 5 Getting ready for the future

Wenn du die Seiten bearbeitet hast, setze ein Häkchen in die Box.

Hello again!
The last day of the holidays

Hello again! We're at the beach. We don't want to go back to school – we want more free time, the summer holidays are too short! ☹

1 Reading and Speaking **Ready for school**

a) *Sieh dir die Fotos an. Lies die Nachrichten der Varndean Kinder. Sind sie froh oder nicht froh zurück in die Schule zu gehen? Umkreise die richtigen Wörter in Blau.*

   1 Lily and Zane are / aren't happy.   2 Noah is / isn't happy.

   3 Sunita is / isn't happy.

b) Walk around *Bist du froh oder nicht froh zurück in der Schule zu sein? Sprecht miteinander.*

> I'm happy. It's nice to see my friends again. What about you?

> I'm not happy. I want to have more free time.

Really? I like school. 😊
I'm at home. I'm wearing my
new school uniform. ✓

I'm in town with my mum. I'm
looking for a new pencil case.
I think school is great! 😍 ✓

2 Listening and Speaking **A day at Brighton beach**

🔊 a) *Stelle dir vor, du bist am Strand. Schließe deine Augen und höre zu.*

🔊 b) *Höre noch einmal zu. Zeichne ein Bild von dir am Strand.*

👥 c) *Zeigt einander eure Bilder. Sprecht darüber.*

I'm looking at the sea.

Some people are swimming.

A boy is eating ice cream.

A girl is playing badminton.

Digital quiz 👆 **Ich kann** über Sommeraktivitäten sprechen.

Unit 1
Travel and holidays

Ms Bond

I was in Spain[1], in a hotel near the beach.

I wasn't away. I was at home in Brighton.

Lily   Noah   Ms Bond

I was in Poland with my mum, but we weren't in a hotel. We were at my aunt and uncle's house.

1 Listening **Where were they?**

a) Before you listen *Sieh dir die Sprechblasen und Fotos oben an. Wo waren Lily, Noah, Ms Bond, Alice, Sunita und Zane? Schreibe die Namen in die Bilder 1–6.*

b) *Höre zu und überprüfe deine Antworten aus a).*

c) *Höre noch einmal zu. Ergänze die Sätze. Ziehe Linien.*

1 Poland: It was warm and it wasn't ...
2 Brighton: It was rainy and ...
3 France: It was hot and ...
4 Wales: It was sometimes ...

cold.

sunny. ☀️

rainy.

windy.

---

[1] **Spain** *Spanien*

○ über meine Ferien sprechen
○ über Ferienaktivitäten schreiben
○ über das letzte Wochenende sprechen
○ von neuen Erfahrungen berichten

Unit task

○ eine Geschichte erzählen

We were on a campsite in Wales.

My mum, my big brother and I were in Prague.

I was in France,
in a holiday apartment.

Alice   Sunita   Zane

2 Speaking **Where were you?**

a) **What were your summer holidays like?** *Wie waren deine Sommerferien?*

1 Where were you?   – I was at home / in a hotel / on a campsite / in ... / ...
2 How was it?   – It was cool / OK / horrible / great / boring / fun / ...
3 What was the weather like? – The weather was nice / OK / hot / cold / rainy /
                                sunny / warm / cloudy / windy / ...

b) Walk around **Ask and answer the questions in a).**
Stelle die Fragen aus a) und beantworte sie.   ▶ Extra practice 1–3, pp. 32–33

Holiday stories

1 Song **My summer holiday**

a) **Listen. Where was the singer?** (Circle) **the correct answer.**
Höre zu. Wo war die Sängerin? Kreise die richtige Antwort ein.

1 Spain   2 France   3 Prague

b) **Listen again.** (Circle) **the correct answer.**
Höre noch einmal zu. Umkreise die richtige Antwort.

1 She was on holiday with her dad and big brother / sister.
2 They stayed in a hotel / apartment.
3 The weather was rainy / hot.
4 They went there by train / car.

Churros – *ein längliches Gebäck aus Spanien/ Portugal*

Erklär-film

2 Looking at language **The simple past**

a) *Sieh dir das Lied an. Wann war der Urlaub?*

It was _____ summer.

Du findest den gesamten Liedtext auf S. 34, Extra Practice 4.

b) *Sieh dir die regelmäßigen Verben im Lied in Blau an. Ergänze die Regel.*

Die einfache Vergangenheit *(simple past)* der regelmäßigen Verben bildest du durch Anhängen von _____ an das Verb.

My summer holiday

I *had* a wonderful[1] holiday last summer!
I *went* to Spain with my dad and my big
   brother.
We *stayed* in a hotel in Granada
And the weather, oh, it *was* hot, hot, hot!
We *went* to Spain and we *went* by train
And we *swam* and *sunbathed* every day.

c) *Lies den Tipp zu den unregelmäßigen Verben. Umkreise sie dann im Lied.*

Manche Verben haben im *simple past* eine unregelmäßige Form:
have – *had,* go – *went,* be – *was / were,* swim – *swam*

▶ Irregular verbs, pp. 170–171

d) *Höre dir das Lied noch einmal an. Stehe bei allen Verben im* simple past *auf.*

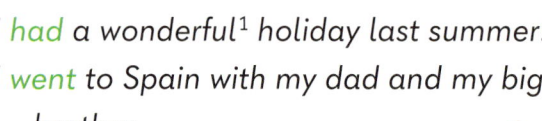

---

[1] **wonderful** *wunderbar*

3 Game **Last summer**

Unterhaltet euch in Gruppen. Eine Person sagt einen Satz aus der Box. Die nächste Person wiederholt den Satz und sagt einen neuen Satz. Ihr könnt auch eigene Sätze bilden. Beispiel:

A Last summer I played basketball.
B Last summer I played basketball and I cycled in the park.

Ideas

I cycled in the park.
I helped my parents.
I listened to music.
I played with my pet.
I watched a lot of films.

4 Noah's summer

Complete Noah's sentences. Use the regular forms of the simple past. *Ergänze Noahs Sätze. Nutze die regelmäßigen Formen des simple past.*

1 I _stayed_____ (stay) in Brighton this summer.

2 I _____ (play) on the beach a lot with Buddy and my cousin.

3 I _____ (watch) films with my parents.

4 I _____ (visit) my grandma in Portsmouth.

▶ **Extra practice 5, p. 34**

5 Sunita and Zane's summer

Match the sentences to the pictures. Write the numbers.
Ordne die Sätze den Bildern zu. Schreibe die Nummern in die Kästchen.

1 We had some pizza.
2 We went to the airport[1] by taxi.
3 I looked after my little sister.
4 My family went to France by car.

[1] **airport** *Flughafen*

6 Reading **A holiday story**

a) Before you read **Where was Sunita on holiday?** (Circle) **the right answer.**
Wo war Sunita im Urlaub? Umkreise die richtige Antwort.

A In Spain   B At home in Brighton
C In Prague

b) **Read Sunita's story. Check your answer from a).** *Lies Sunitas Geschichte. Überprüfe deine Antwort aus a).*

1 My holiday was great! Mum, my brother Nish and I were in Prague. We went by plane and stayed in a hotel. We did a lot of fun activities together.

2 One evening[1] we went on a scary tour in the old town. Our guide looked like a vampire! He told us horrible stories and we were all scared.

3 I had to ask Nish a question, so I put my hand on his arm[2] and said, "Nish?" But I really scared him! He was angry with me.

c) **Read Sunita's story again. Complete the sentences with the words from the box.**
Lies Sunitas Geschichte noch einmal. Ergänze die Sätze mit den Wörtern aus der Box.

1 Sunita and her family went to Prague by *plane* _____.

2 Sunita went on a scary _____.

3 The guide told _____ stories.

4 Sunita really scared _____!

| horrible • Nish • |
| ~~plane~~ • tour |

d) **Do you want to go on a scary tour? Talk to each other.**
Möchtest du auf eine Gruseltour gehen? Redet miteinander.

> I want to go on a scary tour.
> What about you?

> No thanks!
> I don't like scary stories.

[1] **evening** *Abend*   [2] **arm** *Arm*

7 Words **Past activities**

a) **Complete the table with the irregular simple past forms.** *Ergänze die Tabelle mit den unregelmäßigen simple past-Formen.*

did • had • said • told • ~~was/were~~ • went

be	do	go	have	say	tell
was / were	d_ _	w_ _ _ _	h_ _ _	s_ _ _ _	t_ _ _ _

b) **Read the end of Sunita's story. Circle the words in the simple past.** *Lies das Ende von Sunitas Geschichte. Umkreise die Wörter im simple past.*

Nish (was) / is very angry with me! I said / say, "I'm sorry, Nish!" He tell / told me that it was OK. Later he have / had an idea and he did / do something mean: He scared me in the hotel! ▶ Extra practice 6, p. 35 ▶ Irregular verbs, pp. 170–171

8 Words **Travel and holiday words**

Look at the travel and holiday words. Cross out the wrong word under each umbrella. *Sieh dir die Wörter zum Thema Reisen und Urlaub an. Streiche das falsche Wort unter jedem Regenschirm durch.*

 places

 transport

 activities

| hotel, at home, campsite hostel, bus | train, bus, car, park, plane | swim, play games, have ice cream, in France |

My task

9 My summer holidays ▶ Digital help

Lies die Nachricht. Ändere die Wörter in Blau und schreibe eine Nachricht über deine Sommerferien in dein Arbeitsheft. Du kannst die Wörter aus 8 nutzen. Ländernamen findest du auf der Europakarte hinten im Buch. ▶ Wordbank 1, p. 160

Hi!
I was in London with my parents. We went by train. We went shopping and we visited a museum.
Bye!
Tom

At home in the holidays

1 Listening **Time to go to Pride**

a) Before you listen **Lily went to Brighton Pride. Match sentences 1–4 to pictures A–D. Write the numbers.**
Lily ist zur Brighton Pride gegangen. Ordne die Sätze 1–4 den Bildern A–D zu. Schreibe die Nummern in die Kästchen.

Good to know

Pride ist eine große LGBTQ-Parade in Brighton.

   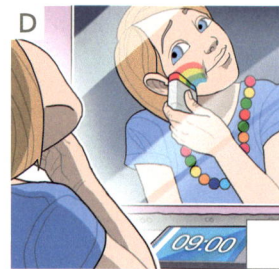

1 Lily got up at seven twenty.
2 She ate breakfast at seven thirty.
3 She made decorations at eight fifteen.
4 She did her Pride make-up at nine o'clock.

b) **The kids are waiting for Sunita at the train station. Listen. Write the platform numbers.** *Die Kinder warten auf Sunita am Bahnhof. Höre zu. Schreibe die Gleisnummern auf.*

from (von)	arrival time (Ankunftszeit)	platform (Gleis)
Cambridge	9.55	4
Eastbourne	10.02	___
London Victoria	10.06	___
Portsmouth	10.11	___
Bristol	10.22	___

2 Viewing **Buying a ticket**

a) Watch the video. (Circle) the right answers.

Sieh dir das Video an. Umkreise die richtigen Antworten.

1 Where does the tourist
   want to go?
   A London   B Cambridge

2 How much is the ticket?
   A £22.50   B £32.50.

3 The tourist thinks the ticket is
   A cheap[1]   B expensive[2]

b) **Complete the dialogue with your answers from a).**

Ergänze den Dialog mit deinen Antworten aus a).

Boy _____ Hi, do you need help?

Tourist __ Yes, please! I need a ticket to _____.

Boy _____ Here you go. It's £ _____.

Tourist __ Oh, that's _____.

Boy _____ Yes, it is.

Tourist __ Thank you!

Boy _____ You're welcome.

c) **Read the dialogue in pairs.**

Lest den Dialog zu zweit.

I can go to London for free!

Good to know	
UK (= United Kingdom) *das Vereinigte Königreich*	**Germany** *Deutschland*
pound (£) *(das Pfund; britische Währung)*	euro (€)
pence	cent

▶ Extra practice 7–8, pp. 35–36

---

[1] **cheap** *billig*   [2] **expensive** *teuer*

3   Reading **Brighton Pride**

Read Lily's messages to her aunt.
Complete the sentences.
Lies Lilys Nachrichten an ihre Tante.
Ergänze die Sätze.

1   Lily went to Pride with her _____.

2   Noah wore his _____.

3   Lily loved all the colours and
    rainbow _____.

4   In the parade they _____
    Willow and her girlfriend.

Pride was so cool 😄 ! I went with my friends. Sunita bought a Pride flag[1] 🏳️‍🌈*, but I didn't buy a flag because I made my own decorations. Noah wore his headphones* 🎧*, so he didn't have a problem with the music. We all wore Pride make-up.* ✓

Erklär-
film

4   Looking at language
        The simple past: negatives

a)   **Complete the sentences.**
        Ergänze die Sätze.

Lily • Noah • The friends • Willow

1   _____ didn't buy a flag.

2   _____ didn't have a
    problem with the music.

3   _____ didn't see Lily.

4   _____ didn't go to the
    concert.

b)   *Sieh dir die Sätze in a) an. Wie*
        verneinst du eine Aussage im
        simple past? Setze das richtige Wort ein.

        Ich verneine eine Aussage im
        simple past immer mit _____
        und dem Verb im Infinitiv (z. B.
        buy, have, see).

We watched the parade. It was so fun, and everybody was really happy! I loved all the colours and rainbow 🌈 *clothes. We saw Willow in the parade with her girlfriend[2], but they didn't see us.* ✓

Then we ate rainbow cake 🍰*. We didn't go to the concert after the parade, but we listened to street musicians* 🎸 *. We had a great time!* ✓

---

[1] **flag** *Flagge*   [2] **girlfriend** *(feste) Freundin*

5 A message from Lily's aunt

Lily's aunt Svetlana texted her back. Put the blue words in the simple past (negative). *Lilys Tante Svetlana schreibt zurück. Setze die blauen Wörter in das simple past (negative).*

I love your photos, Lily! We <u>didn't have</u> *(1 not have) a Pride festival here. We went to a music festival, but I* <u>didn't</u> *(2 not like) the music! The bands* _____ *(3 not play) my kind of music. We* _____ *(4 not stay) very long and went home.* ✓

▶ Extra practice 9, p. 36

6 Julia didn't …

Choose the right ending for each sentence. Draw lines.
Wähle das richtige Ende für jeden Satz. Ziehe Linien.

1 Julia didn't play	a swimming.
2 Amir didn't watch	b pizza.
3 Laura didn't eat	c tennis.
4 Bez didn't go	d TV.

My task

7 My town in the holidays

▶ Digital help

a) *Schreibe vier Sätze über den letzten Sommer in dein Arbeitsheft. Schreibe zwei wahre Sätze und zwei unwahre Sätze. Du kannst die Ideen in der Box oder deine eigenen Ideen nutzen.*

> played video games • had ice cream • saw a film • didn't do homework • went to the beach • didn't go swimming • had a great summer

b) *Tauscht eure Sätze untereinander aus. Macht ein Häkchen (✓) an die wahren Sätze und ein Kreuz (✗) an die unwahren.*

c) *Überprüft gemeinsam eure Antworten. Sind sie richtig?*

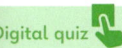 **Ich kann** über einen besonderen Tag in meinen Ferien sprechen. twenty-one **21**

A weekend project

1 Listening **Welcome, Finn!**

a) Before you listen **Look at the photo. Who is Finn? Circle the right answer.**
Sieh dir das Foto an. Wer ist Finn? Umkreise die richtige Antwort.

Finn is a new student / parent / teacher.

b) **Listen and circle the right answer.**
Höre zu und umkreise die richtige Antwort.

He's really cute!

name	Finn Demir / Lily Demir
from	Dresden / Prague
pet	dog / cat
likes	computers / parkour

c) **Listen again and check.** *Höre noch einmal zu und überprüfe.*

2 Mediation **A silent disco beach clean-up**

a) *Frau Bond erzählt der Klasse 8C von einem Klassenprojekt. Lies den Flyer.*

Come to our silent disco clean-up on Brighton beach!

- Collect rubbish and listen to music!
- Wear cool clothes.
- And bring headphones!

b) *Finn erzählt seiner Mutter zu Hause von der Säuberungsaktion am Strand. Ergänze.*

Finn   Am Samstag wollen wir

_____.

Mutter   Klingt super! Was sollst du dafür anziehen?

Finn   _____.

Mutter   Sollst du etwas mitbringen?

Finn   _____.

3 Listening On Monday

a) *Nach der Säuberungsaktion am Strand spricht Frau Bond mit der Klasse. Höre zu und sieh dir die Bilder an. Die Kinder haben eine Sache nicht gefunden. Streiche sie durch (✗).*

A
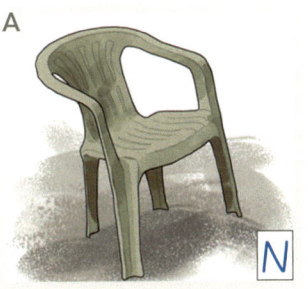
N

B

C
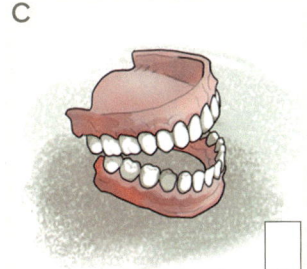

D

E
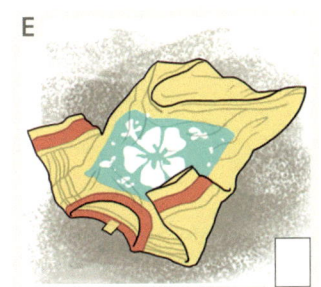

F

b) *Höre noch einmal zu. Schreibe S (Sunita), N (Noah), F (Finn) oder L (Lily) in die Kästchen bei den Sachen, die sie gefunden haben.*

My task

4 Last weekend

a) *Schreibe über dein letztes Wochenende. Du kannst die Wörter in der Box oder deine eigenen Ideen nutzen.*

> played video games • saw my friends • helped my dad • watched TV •
> didn't go shopping • didn't make my bed • ...

1 Last weekend I _____.

2 At lunchtime on Saturday I _____.

3 On Sunday at 12.30 I _____.

4 On Sunday at 6 o'clock I _____.

b) Speed dating *Erzähle anderen von deinem letzten Wochenende. Lies deine Sätze vor.*

▶ Extra practice 10, p. 37

Noah's adventure

1   Reading   **Noah's journey**

a)   Before you read **Look at Noah's ticket and** 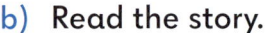 **the right words.**
Sieh dir Noahs Fahrkarte an und umkreise die richtigen Wörter.

   1   Noah travelled[1] on Saturday / Sunday.

   2   He travelled from Brighton to London / Portsmouth.

   3   He travelled at 8:45 / 9:45.

   4   He travelled by plane / train.

b)   **Read the story.**
Lies die Geschichte.

Saturday 5th October

   1   Today I travelled to my grandma's house alone for the first time. I love seeing my grandma, but she lives in Portsmouth.

   2   Last week Sunita asked me, "Do you want to see her alone?" I thought about it and I was scared at first. But then I thought, "I want to try!"

   3   So this morning dad bought a ticket for me and Buddy and I got on the train at Brighton station.

   4   I had a great day with grandma in Portsmouth. We had a picnic and Buddy swam in the sea – he was so happy! Grandma and I were happy too.

   5   In the afternoon Grandma and I were tired, so Grandma took me to Portsmouth station. But there was a problem – I got on the wrong train! I was really scared at first, and I didn't know what to do!

---

[1] **travel** *reisen*

20 6 Then Buddy looked at me. He was very calm and he helped me to feel calm too. I texted Sunita, Lily and Zane and they helped me find the right train back to Brighton.

7 I texted Mum and Dad too and I told them what happened. They were really proud of me for trying something new. I was proud too!

2 What happened?

Put what happened in the right order.
Bringe die Ereignisse in die richtige Reihenfolge.

	Buddy swam in the sea.
1	Sunita talked to Noah about his grandma.
	Noah's friends helped him.
	Noah got the right train to Brighton.
	Noah got on the wrong train.
	Noah got the train to Portsmouth.

3 Feelings in the story

Find the blue words in the story. Complete the table with the right word.
Finde die blauen Wörter in der Geschichte. Ergänze die Tabelle mit den passenden Wörtern.

	Feeling (Gefühl)	Name
1	= scared	Noah
2	_____	Buddy, grandma, Noah

	Feeling (Gefühl)	Name
3	_____	Buddy, Noah
4	_____	mum, dad, Noah

▶ Extra practice 11–14, pp. 37–38

4 Showtime **Scenes from Noah's story**

a) Who maybe said these sentences? (Circle) the correct
names. *Wer sagte vielleicht diese Sätze? Umkreise die
richtigen Namen.*

1 I want to see my grandma more, but she
lives in Portsmouth.   Noah / Noah's dad

– Do you want to see her alone?   Noah / Sunita

2 Welcome to Portsmouth, Noah!
It's so nice to see you!   grandma / Sunita

– I'm so happy to be here, Grandma!   Noah's friends / Noah

3 Oh no, I'm on the wrong train!
I don't know what to do!   Sunita / Noah

– Don't be scared, Noah. Get off
the train at the next station.   Noah's friends / grandma

b) In groups, act out the scenes from **a)**. *Spielt die Szenen aus a) in Gruppen vor.*

5 Life skills **Try new things**

a) Look at the activities. Are they scary for you? Write **yes** or **no**.
Sieh dir die Aktivitäten an. Machen sie dir Angst? Schreibe yes oder no.

1 singing to other people	_____	4 sitting in a dark room	_____
2 picking up[1] a snake	_____	5 talking to new people	_____
3 travelling by plane	_____	6 talking in front of the class	_____

b) What new things do you want to try this year? Tell each other at least one thing.
Was möchtest du dieses Jahr ausprobieren? Erzählt einander mindestens eine Sache.

> *I want to try …*

---

[1] **pick up** *hochheben*

Digital quiz **Ich kann über neue Erfahrungen sprechen.** ✓

Brighton stories: Summer holidays

Gloria Daisy Emir Joe

1 Holiday places

Before you watch **Where do you want to go on holiday? Why? Write and use the words from the box. Then tell each other.** *Wohin möchtest du gerne in den Ferien fahren? Warum? Schreibe es auf und nutze die Wörter in der Box. Erzählt es dann einander.*

hot • fun • interesting • different • nice to see my grandmother / cousin ... • cool • sunny

I'd like to go to _____ because it's _____.

2 Viewing **Three holiday experiences**

a) **Watch part 1. Who stayed in Brighton for the holidays?**
Sieh dir Teil 1 an. Wer ist in den Ferien in Brighton geblieben? _____

b) **Watch part 2. Are the sentences true (✓) or false (✗)?**
Sieh dir Teil 2 an. Sind die Sätze richtig (✓) oder falsch (✗)?

1	Gloria has a great idea.	☐	3 Joe chooses[2] the best garden.	☐
2	Daisy, Emir and Gloria want to act out[1] their holidays for Joe.	☐	4 Joe wants to go on holiday with Daisy.	☐

c) **Watch part 3. Put the pictures in the right order. Write 1–3.**
Sieh dir Teil 3 an. Bringe die Bilder in die richtige Reihenfolge. Schreibe 1–3.

d) **Watch part 4. Whose holiday did Joe like the best?** (Circle) **the picture in c).**
Sieh dir Teil 4 an. Welche Ferien fand Joe am besten? Umkreise das Bild in c).

---

[1] **Scotland** *Schottland*

Plan a story

1   Give the story a structure

Decide: Are these sentences best for the beginning, middle or end of a story? Draw lines. *Entscheide: Sind diese Sätze am besten am Anfang, in der Mitte oder am Ende einer Geschichte? Ziehe Linien.*

1 Then I walked to my friend's house.	beginning (Anfang)
2 So in the end we were happy!	middle (mittlerer Teil)
3 Last week something funny happened.	end (Ende)

2   Make the story interesting

Complete the sentences with the words from the box. *Ergänze die Sätze mit Wörtern aus der Box.*

black • new • green • ~~sunny~~

Verwende Adjektive, um deine Sätze interessanter zu machen: *Scout is a cool seagull!*

1   It was a warm, *sunny*   day.

2   I saw a big, _____ dog.

3   It went into a nice, _____ garden.

4   I saw that my _____ phone was missing[1]. Oh no!

3   Link the sentences

Complete the sentences. Circle the right word. *Ergänze die Sätze. Umkreise das richtige Wort.*

Mit *linking words (and, but)* verbindest du zwei Sätze miteinander:
- *Scout is clever and she's nice.*
- *Scout likes dogs, but she doesn't like cats.*

1   I thought hard   (and) / but   I looked in all my bags.

2   I looked in the street again,   and / but   I didn't find my phone.

3   I went to my friend's house   and / but   I told her the story.

4   She was very sad,   and / but   then I saw the big dog with my phone!

[1] **missing** *verschwunden*

Digital quiz 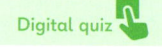   **Ich kann** eine Geschichte planen.

Tell a story

Step 1

a) *Lest die Geschichte.*

b) *Findet sieben Adjektive in der Geschichte. Unterstreicht sie.*

c) *Findet drei Verbindungswörter. Umkreist sie.*

Last summer I wanted a new bike, (but) I didn't have the money.

I sold[1] some old things, but I needed more money. I was sad.

Then my sister told me about a cheap bike! It was at a small shop near our flat and the shop was still open. I went to the shop.

In the end I got a new bike! I was very happy and I told my sister, "Thank you!"
I had a great summer.

Step 2

 ▶ Digital help

Verändert die Wörter in Blau und schreibt eine neue Geschichte in euer Arbeitsheft.

Step 3

Übt den Text laut zu lesen. Nehmt den Text mit einem Handy auf.

---

[1] **sell** (*simple past:* **sold**) *verkaufen*

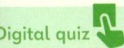 **Ich kann** eine Geschichte erzählen.

1   Speaking   **Where were you, Finn?**   Ich kann über die Ferien und das Wetter sprechen.

Finn tells his class about his holiday. Complete his sentences with *was* or *were*.
Finn erzählt seiner Klasse über seine Ferien. Ergänze die Sätze mit was *oder* were.

Hi, everybody.

Bavaria – Germa

I _was_ in Bavaria in Germany.

my dad

I _____ with my dad.

the campsite

We _____ on a campsite.

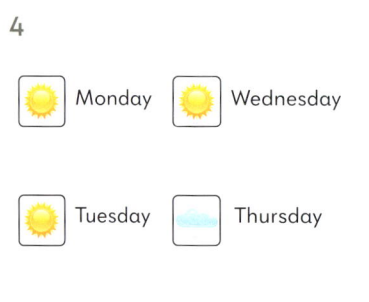

Monday   Wednesday
Tuesday   Thursday

The weather _____ sunny and cloudy.

the holiday

The holiday _____ great!

2   **A really good holiday**   Ich kann über meine Ferienaktivitäten schreiben *(simple past)*.

Language   **Read Lily's message to Alice about her holiday. Write the verbs in the simple past. The blue words are regular. The green verbs are irregular.** *Lies Lilys Nachricht über ihre Ferien an Alice. Setze die Verben ins* simple past. *Die blauen Wörter sind regelmäßig. Die grünen Wörter sind unregelmäßig.*

> Hi Alice! I _had_ (have) a great time in Poland. We _____ (stay) at my aunt Svetlana's house. We _____ (do) a lot of fun activities together. I love that city. I _____ (take) some great photos! And I _____ (play) computer games with my uncle. How was Wales? Lily

Check

3 Language **An interesting day**

Lies Noahs Gespräch mit seiner Mutter. Ergänze die Sätze mit den Wörtern in der Box.

> ~~didn't eat~~ • didn't walk • didn't watch • didn't wear

Mum ___ Hi, Noah, how was your day at Pride?

Noah ___ It was great! I *didn't eat* sandwiches, I ate rainbow cake. I _____ a grey T-shirt, I wore a green T-shirt and a lot of different colours. I _____ TV, I watched a parade. And people _____ in the streets, they danced!

Mum ___ Wow, you had a great day!

4 Mediation **An interview with Finn**

Lies einen Ausschnitt aus dem Interview mit Finn in der Onlinezeitung TeenZine. Sein Großvater stellt ihm dazu einige Fragen am Telefon. Ergänze Finns Antworten.

www.varndean-teen-zine-online.example.com

A new student's first weeks at Varndean

TeenZine Finn, tell us about your first weeks at our school. What were your highlights?

Finn I really liked the dance lesson in PE. And some of my new friends said my English is good. I'm proud of that!

TeenZine I think you can be very proud of that!

Opa ___ Gestern hast du mir dein Online-Interview geschickt. Worum ging es da?

Finn ___ Es ging um _____.

Opa ___ Und was hat dir bis jetzt am besten gefallen?

Finn ___ _____ im Sportunterricht.

Und einige meiner neuen Freunde sagten, _____

_____.

Opa ___ Das hört sich ja toll an!

Check

▶ page 13

Extra practice 1

a) **Put a tick (✓) next to words for places.**

Mache ein Häkchen (✓) bei den Wörtern, die einen Ort beschreiben.

1 swimming pool ☐   2 my friend's house ☐   3 rainy ☐

4 home ☐   5 supermarket ☐   6 school ☐

7 holiday ☐   8 shopping centre ☐   9 afternoon ☐

b) **Make a circle. Throw a ball and say where you were yesterday.**

Stellt euch im Kreis auf. Werft einen Ball und sagt, wo ihr gestern wart.

I was at the swimming pool. Where were you?

I wasn't at the swimming pool. I was at the supermarket. Where were you?

▶ page 13

Extra practice 2

👥 a) **Walk around Ask the questions. Can you find a person for each question? Write the names.** *Stelle die Fragen. Finde jemanden für jede Frage. Schreibe die Namen auf.*

1 Were you by the sea?

_____

2 Were you at the cinema?

_____

3 Were you in a hot country?

_____

4 Were you in another country?

_____

5 Were you on a day trip?

_____

6 Were you in the mountains[1]?

_____

Were you by the sea?

No, I wasn't. Were you at the cinema?

Yes, I was.

Great!

b) **When you have six names, say "Here!"**
Wenn du sechs Namen hast, sage „Here!".

Extra practice 3

▶ page 13

Complete the sentences with was or were.
Ergänze die Sätze mit was *oder* were.

Lily _____   Where *were* _____ you in the summer

holidays? _____ you in Brighton?

Beni _____   No, I _____ in France with my family.

We _____ there for three weeks.

Lily _____   How _____ it?

Beni _____   It _____ cool!

---

[1] **mountain** *Berg*

▶ page 14

Extra practice 4

Listen to the song. *Höre dir das Lied an.*

My summer holiday

I had a wonderful holiday last summer!
I went to Spain with my dad and my big brother.
We stayed in a hotel in Granada
and the weather, oh, it was hot, hot, hot!

We went to Spain and we went by train
and we swam and sunbathed[1] every[2] day.
It was so cool in the swimming pool!
It was the best ever holiday! ¡Olé!

We watched flamenco dancers in the street,
we listened and danced[3] and moved[4] our feet[5].
I loved eating churros, hot and sweet,
and the tapas, oh, they were oh-so good!

We went to Spain ...

[1] **sunbathe** *sonnenbaden*
[2] **every** *jede (r,s)*
[3] **dance** *tanzen*
[4] **move** *bewegen*
[5] **feet** *Füße*

▶ page 15

Extra practice 5

Find the words in the box. Circle them.
Finde die Wörter in der Box. Umkreise sie.

helped • ~~played~~ •
stayed • visited • watched

P	L	A	Y	E	D	A	U
D	P	J	G	X	F	Z	V
W	T	S	W	Y	R	E	I
A	Y	T	M	T	F	K	S
T	F	A	Z	R	F	X	I
C	X	Y	E	S	L	E	T
H	F	E	E	D	O	Z	E
E	W	D	X	Y	I	S	D
D	H	E	L	P	E	D	I

Extra practice 6

▶ page 17

Write the verbs in blue in the simple past.
Setze die blauen Verben ins simple past.

My summer
by Ringo

I *stayed* (stay) in Brighton this summer,
but you know what?
I ________ (have) a great time!
My friend Brandon and I ________ (do) a lot of
fun things together.
We went swimming, ________ (eat) ice cream
and played football.

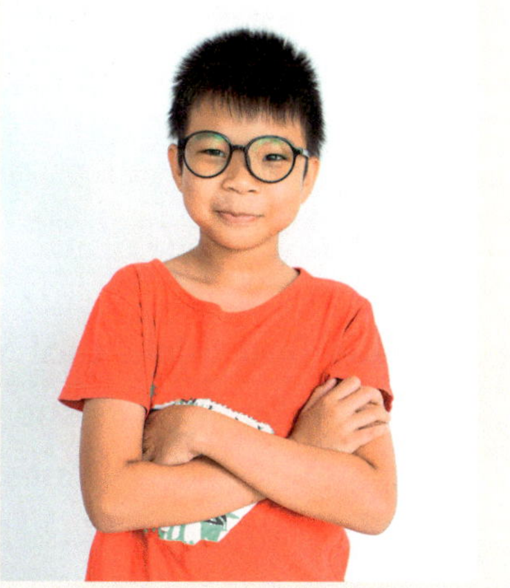

I always ________ (go) to bed late and my dad and I often ________ (make) pizza at home. I love pizza! It ________ (be) a really good summer.

Extra practice 7

▶ page 19

Match the sentences to the words. Draw lines.
Ordne die Sätze den Wörtern zu. Ziehe Linien.

1 It's a place to stay. It's like a hotel.	a train
2 It's a kind of car. It takes you to places for money.	b dancing
3 It's an activity. You often do it when there is music.	c hostel
4 It's a place to stay. You don't have a room.	d taxi
5 People get on it at a station. It's very fast.	e campsite

▶ page 19

Extra practice 8

Complete the sentences with the words from the box.
Ergänze die Sätze mit den Wörtern aus der Box.

5 o'clock • London • ~~station~~ • ticket

1 Brighton has a big train *station* .

2 This is the train to _____ .

3 My train is at _____ .

4 I need a _____ to Brighton, please.

Extra practice 9

▶ page 21

Blue Bird thinks that Scout did some bad things at Pride. Scout says she didn't do them. Match their sentences. Draw lines.
Blue Bird denkt, dass Scout ein paar dumme Sachen bei der Pride Parade gemacht hat. Scout sagt, sie hätte das nicht getan. Ordne die Sätze einander zu. Ziehe Linien.

OK, maybe[1] I ate all the chips ...

Blue Bird	Scout
1 You ate all the chips!	a No, I didn't! I wore my favourite red hat.
2 You played bad music!	b No, I didn't. Some teenagers played bad music.
3 You wore my Pride hat!	c No, I didn't. That was Green Bird! He played on his phone.
4 You played on your phone at the concert!	d No, I didn't. Black Bird ate all the chips!

---

[1] **maybe** *vielleicht*

Extra practice 10 ▶ page 23

a) Put the time phrases in the right order. Start with today and go back in time.
Bringe die Zeitwörter in die richtige Reihenfolge. Beginne mit today und gehe in der Zeit zurück.

last weekend ☐ today ⟦1⟧ yesterday[1] ⟦2⟧ last week ☐ last month[2] ⟦5⟧ last year ☐

b) Write the phrases from a) in the correct order.
Schreibe die Begriffe aus a) in der richtigen Reihenfolge.

1 *today* _____

2 _____

3 _____

4 _____

5 _____

6 _____

c) Bildet Gruppen. Seht euch die Zeitwörter an. Jede Person wählt einen Begriff. Stellt euch in einer Reihe in der richtigen Reihenfolge auf. Beginnt mit today und geht rückwärts in der zeitlichen Reihenfolge der Begriffe.

Extra practice 11 ▶ page 25

Read the sentences. Tick (✓) the right sentences. *Lies die Sätze. Mache ein Häkchen (✓) neben den richtigen Sätzen.*

1 Noah often goes to his grandma's house alone. ☐

2 Noah's grandma lives in Portsmouth. ✓

3 Noah's dad bought the ticket for Noah. ☐

4 Noah and his grandma swam in the sea. ☐

5 Noah got on the wrong train. ☐

6 Noah took the bus back to Brighton. ☐

7 Noah's parents were angry with Noah. ☐

---

[1] **yesterday** *gestern*   [2] **month** *Monat*

Extra practice 12 ▶ page 25

Draw lines. *Ziehe Linien.*

1 scared •		• a *froh*
2 happy •		• b *stolz*
3 calm •		• c *ängstlich*
4 proud •		• d *ruhig*

Extra practice 13 ▶ page 25

Am Montag sprechen Sunita und Noah über Noahs Reise nach Portsmouth. Ziehe Linien von den Fragen zu den richtigen Antworten.

1 Sunita _ Hi Noah! Did you get home OK on Saturday?	a Noah _ No, he didn't. Buddy swam in the sea. He loved it!
2 Sunita _ That's ok. Was it nice to see your grandma?	b Noah _ We went to the beach. Then we had a picnic.
3 Sunita _ What did you do with your grandma?	c Noah _ Yes, we had a great time.
4 Sunita _ And did Buddy eat sandwiches too?	d Noah _ Yes, I do!
5 Sunita _ It was a perfect day. Do you want to visit her again?	e Noah _ Yes, I did. Thanks for helping me.

Extra practice 14 ▶ page 25

Lies die Sätze. Umkreise das richtige blaue Wort.

1 One day Zane, Holly and Eno went to the beach, and /(but) they didn't go swimming.

2 At first, Holly was unhappy, and / but then Eno bought ice cream.

3 They walked together on the beach and / but watched the sea.

4 "This was fun, and / but I'm cold. I want to go home to see mum now," said Zane.

5 They went home and / but Eno made pizza for dinner. It was great!

Hello again!

▶ p. 10 **more** — mehr, weitere

summer holidays — die Sommerferien

again — wieder, noch einmal

▶ p. 11 **(to) wear** — tragen, anhaben *(Kleidung)*

sea — das Meer, die See

ice cream — das (Speise-)Eis

Ice cream on a warm day – great!

Unit 1: Travel and holidays

▶ p. 12 I **was** ... — Ich **war** ...
We **were** ... — Wir **waren** ...

	I am	I was
•	**I am** ich bin	**I was** ich war
•	**he/she/it is** er/sie/es ist	**he/she/it was** er/sie/es war

I **wasn't** (= was not) ... — Ich war nicht ...
They **weren't** (= were not) — Sie waren nicht ...
...

•	**we are** wir sind	**we were** wir waren
•	**you are** du bist; ihr seid	**you were** du warst; ihr wart
•	**they are** sie sind	**they were** sie waren

away — weg, fort

Ms Bond — Frau Bond

warm — warm

cold — kalt

YES	NO
I was	I wasn't
you were	you weren't
he/she/it was	he/she/it wasn't
we were	we weren't
you were	you weren't
they were	they weren't

▶ p. 13 **campsite** — der Campingplatz

Prague — Prag

holiday apartment — die Ferienwohnung

Topic 1

▶ p. 14 **on holiday** — im Urlaub

(to) stay — übernachten; bleiben
they stayed — sie übernachteten, sie haben übernachtet; sie blieben, sie sind geblieben

(to) go: they went — sie gingen, sie sind gegangen

last summer — (im) letzten Sommer

(to) have: I had — ich hatte, ich habe gehabt

(to) swim: I swam — ich schwamm, ich bin geschwommen

| ▶ p. 16 | plane | das Flugzeug |
| | | |

a plane

	(to) do: he **did**	machen, tun: er machte/tat; er hat gemacht/getan
	fun	lustig
	scary	unheimlich, beängstigend, gruselig
	guide	der Fremdenführer / die Fremdenführerin
	vampire	der Vampir
	(to) tell: he **told**	erzählen: er erzählte, er hat erzählt
	story	die Geschichte (*Erzählung*)
	(to) say: they **said**	sagen: sie sagten; sie haben gesagt
▶ p. 17	He told me **that** ...	Er sagte mir, **dass** ...
	something	etwas

Topic 2

▶ p. 18	pride	der Stolz (*Pride (oder die Pride Parade) ist ein Demonstrationstag von Lesben, Schwulen, Bisexuellen und Transgender-Personen*)
	(to) get up: she **got up**	aufstehen: sie stand auf; sie ist aufgestanden
	(to) eat: she **ate**	essen: sie aß; sie hat gegessen
	(to) make: I **made**	machen: ich machte, ich habe gemacht
	decoration	der Dekoration, der Schmuck, die Verzierung
▶ p. 19	cheap	billig, preiswert
	expensive	teuer
▶ p. 20	(to) wear: he **wore** ...	tragen, anhaben (*Kleidung*): er trug ... / er hatte ... an; er hat ... getragen, er hat ... angehabt
	rainbow	der Regenbogen
	parade	die Parade, der Umzug
	(to) buy: she **bought**	kaufen: sie kaufte; sie hat gekauft
	I **didn't** buy ... (= **did not**)	ich kaufte nicht, ich habe nicht gekauft
	my own decorations	meine eigene Dekoration, mein eigener Schmuck
	(to) see: they **saw**	sehen: sie sahen; sie haben gesehen
	concert	das Konzert

I bought ◀ ▶ I didn't buy

| street | die Straße *(in Ortschaften)* |
| musician | der Musiker, die Musikerin |

Topic 3

▶ p. 22 | silent | still, lautlos |

Story

▶ p. 24
(to) travel	reisen, fahren
today	heute
(to) think: I **thought**	denken: ich dachte, ich habe gedacht
(to) **try**, *past tense:* **tried**	versuchen, (aus)probieren
morning	der Morgen
(to) **get on** (a train/bus), *past tense:* **got on**	einsteigen (in einen Zug/Bus)
afternoon	der Nachmittag
I didn't **know** what to do.	Ich wusste nicht, was ich tun sollte.

▶ p. 25
calm	ruhig, besonnen
(to) **text** sb.	jm. eine SMS schicken
(to) **happen** (**to** sb.)	(jm.) geschehen, passieren
proud (of)	stolz (auf)

▶ p. 26
| (to) **get off** (a train/bus), *past tense:* **got off** | aussteigen (aus einem Zug/Bus) |
| dark | dunkel |

Study skills

▶ p. 28 | **into** a garden | in einen Garten (hinein) |

Irregular verbs

(to) **be**	was/were	*sein*	(to) **make**	made	*machen*
(to) **buy**	bought	*kaufen*	(to) **put**	put	*legen, stellen*
(to) **do**	did	*machen, tun*	(to) **say**	said	*sagen*
(to) **eat**	ate	*essen*	(to) **see**	saw	*sehen*
(to) **get**	got	*bekommen*	(to) **swim**	swam	*schwimmen*
(to) **go**	went	*gehen, fahren*	(to) **tell**	told	*erzählen*
(to) **do**	did	*machen, tun*	(to) **think**	thought	*denken*
(to) **eat**	ate	*essen*	(to) **try**	tried	*ausprobieren*
(to) **have**	had	*haben*	(to) **wear**	wore	*tragen, anhanben*

Unit 2
Friends and heroes

A

brown eyes

B

short,
straight hair

1 Listening **The head students**

a) *Höre zu. Was ist das richtige Bild für jedes Kind? Schreibe A–D.*

1 Jodie has brown eyes and a blue-green tie.	A
2 Faye has long, curly hair and glasses.	___
3 Mihai has short, straight, blond hair and a red tie.	___
4 Sofia has braces and brown hair.	___

b) *Höre noch einmal zu und überprüfe.*

Nach dieser Unit kann ich ...

○ Aussehen beschreiben
○ die Persönlichkeit meiner Freundinnen und Freunde beschreiben
○ über meine Vorbilder sprechen
○ einen Superhelden oder eine Superheldin beschreiben
○ über Zusammenarbeit sprechen

Unit task ✓

○ Informationen recherchieren und ein Quiz erstellen

C

long, curly hair

D

glasses

braces

2 Speaking **What do they look like?**

a) *Schreibe über eine Person in deiner Klasse. Du kannst die Wörter aus 1 nutzen.*

My person has _____ hair and _____ eyes.

My person (has / doesn't have) _____.

b) Game *Lies deine Sätze der Klasse vor. Erraten die Kinder deine Person? Errätst du andere Personen?*

My friends

1 Reading **The poster competition**

a) Before you read *Wie ist ein guter Freund / eine gute Freundin? Umkreise die Eigenschaft, die dir am wichtigsten ist. Erzählt es einander.*

A good friend is funny / cool / interesting.

b) *Die Kinder machen Poster über ihre Freunde und Freundinnen. Wer wird in A und B beschrieben: Lily, Zane, Sunita oder Noah?*

A _____   B _____

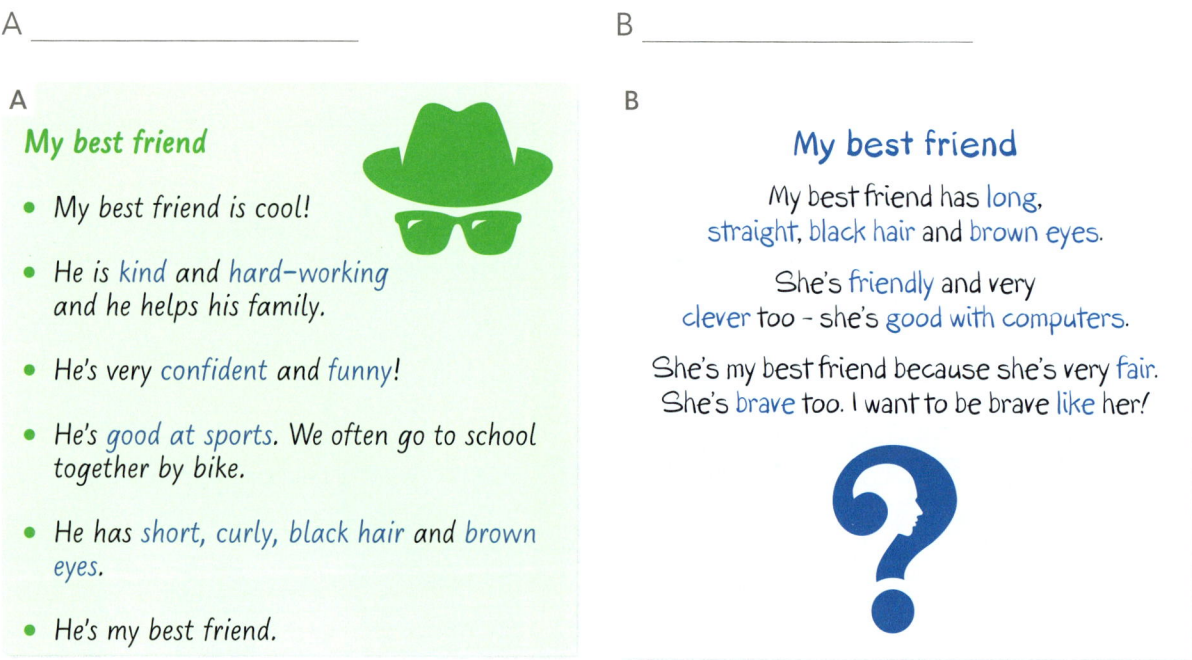

A

My best friend

- My best friend is cool!

- He is kind and hard-working and he helps his family.

- He's very confident and funny!

- He's good at sports. We often go to school together by bike.

- He has short, curly, black hair and brown eyes.

- He's my best friend.

B

My best friend

My best friend has long, straight, black hair and brown eyes.

She's friendly and very clever too – she's good with computers.

She's my best friend because she's very fair. She's brave too. I want to be brave like her!

c) **Listen and check your answers.** *Höre zu und überprüfe deine Antworten.*

d) *Ergänze die Mindmap. Nutze auch die blauen Wörter in b) und die Wörter in den Fotos auf den Seiten 42–43. Du kannst eine große Mindmap in dein Heft zeichnen.*

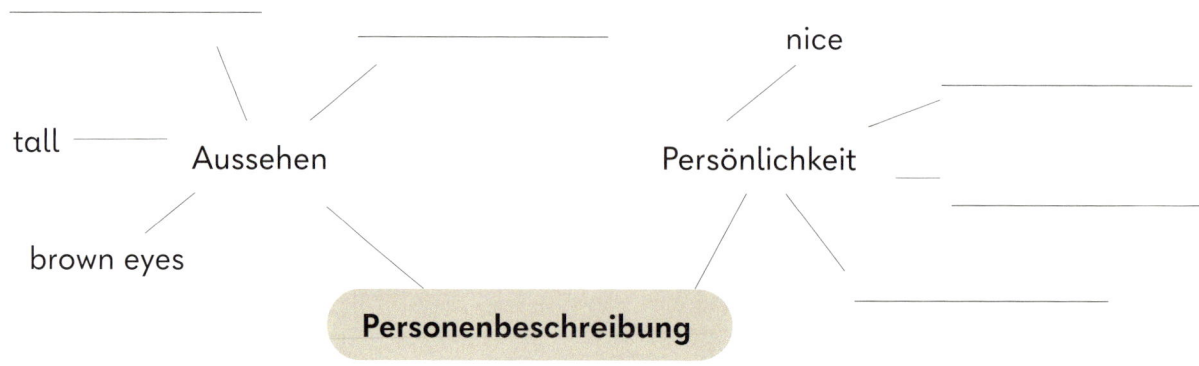

_____

nice

_____

tall ——— Aussehen   Persönlichkeit _____

brown eyes

Personenbeschreibung

_____

▶ Wordbank 2, p. 161   ▶ Extra practice 1, p. 65

2 Speaking **I think you're ...**

a) **What are nice things that you can say to other people? Write sentences.**
Welche netten Sachen kannst du anderen Menschen sagen? Schreibe Sätze auf.

brave • clever • confident • funny •
good at sports / ... • hard-working • helpful • nice

I'm clever! I'm funny! I'm good at flying!

I think you're nice.

Thank you. I think you're helpful.

Sei auch nett zu dir selbst!

I think you're

_____.

_____

b) Double circle **Say something nice to each other.** *Sagt einander etwas Nettes.*

3 Words **Personality words**

a) *Was ist dir an einem Freund / einer Freundin wichtig? Umkreise drei Wörter in der Box. Erzählt einander eure Ergebnisse.*

brave • clever • confident • cool • funny • good at sports • hard-working •
helpful • nice

b) *Was ist dir wichtig an deiner Lehrkraft? Schreibe drei Wörter auf. Erzählt einander eure Ergebnisse.*

_____, _____, _____

c) *Mache ein Poster über eine perfekte Person: Freund/Freundin, Lehrkraft, Sportler/ Sportlerin oder Popstar. Wie sollten die Person sein?*

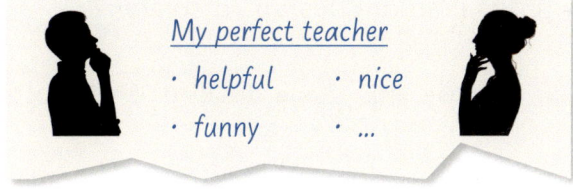

My perfect teacher
· helpful   · nice
· funny   · ...

4 Song No one else like you

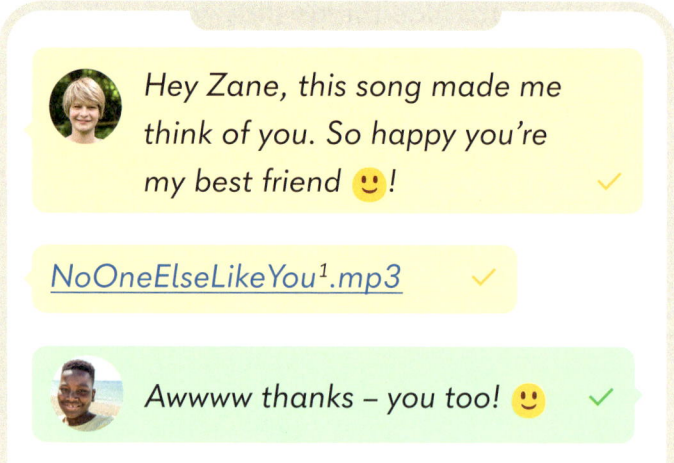

Hey Zane, this song made me think of you. So happy you're my best friend 🙂!

NoOneElseLikeYou[1].mp3

Awwww thanks – you too! 🙂

a) Before you listen **Read the messages and complete the sentences.**
Lies die Nachrichten und ergänze die Sätze.

1 Lily sent a _____ to Noah.   2 Lily is _____ because they are best friends!

b) **Listen to the song. Complete the lines with the pictures. Draw lines.**
Höre das Lied an. Vervollständige die Zeilen mit den Bildern. Ziehe Linien.

No one else like you[1]

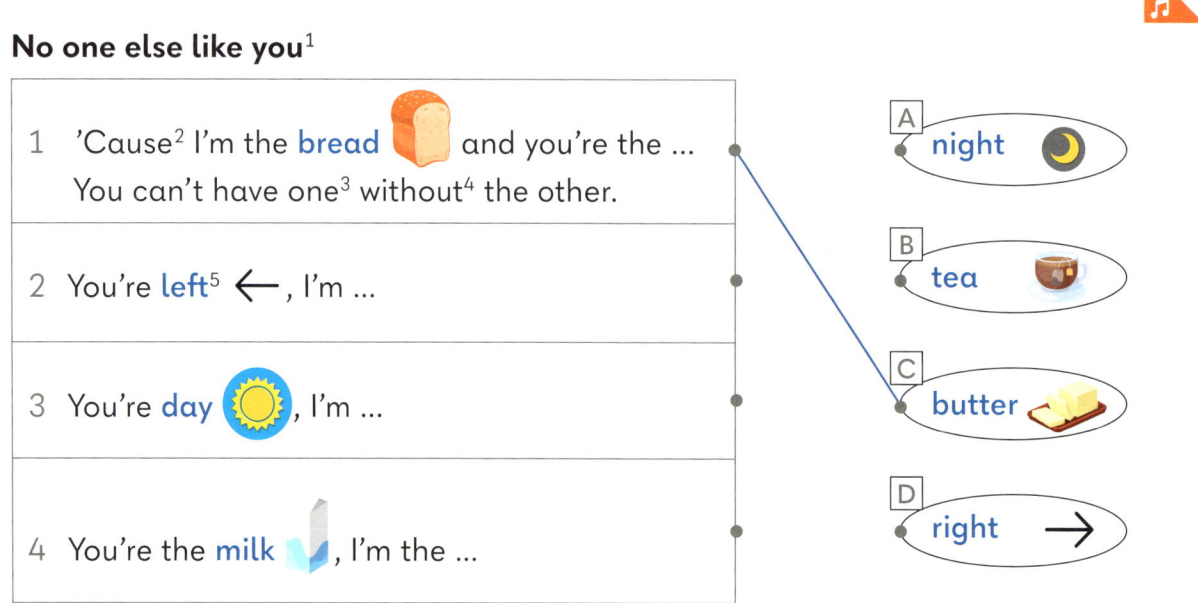

c) **Listen to the song again. Sing or mime. Have a competition with your class. Who can mime the best?** *Höre das Lied noch einmal. Singe mit oder spiele es vor. Macht in der Klasse einen Wettbewerb. Wer kann das Lied am besten vorspielen?*

---

[1] **no one else like you** *es gibt niemanden wie dich* [2] **'cause** *weil* [3] **one** *das Eine* [4] **without** *ohne*
[5] **left** *links*

5 Mediation **Finn's friend**

a) *Lies Finns Nachrichten. An wen schreibt er? Umkreise die beiden Namen.*

b) *Sieh dir Sunitas Fragen 1–3 an. Beantworte ihre Fragen auf Englisch.*

> Hi, Suri! Ich hab schon *viele Freunde* an meiner neuen Schule. 🙂 Neben mir sitzt Noah. Er hat *einen Hund*, der heißt Buddy. In meiner Klasse ist auch ein *cooles und witziges Mädchen*. 🎧 Sie heißt Sunita.
> LG Finn

> ???

> 😐 Sorry, Sunita, that message wasn't for you! It was for a friend in Germany.

1 *Freunde* is in English *friends*, I think. What does he say about friends?
   – He says that he has _____.

2 He writes something about Noah. What does he say about him?
   – He says that Noah has _____.

3 He talks about me too! What does he say about me?
   – He says that you are _____.

My task

6 **My favourite person** ▶ Digital help 📱

a) *Mache ein Poster über deine Lieblingsperson. Ändere die Wörter in Blau. Du kannst auch ein Bild dazu zeichnen.*

My favourite person has green eyes and black hair. He has glasses.	blue • brown • blond • red • …
My favourite person is great because he's funny and helpful.	brave • clever • confident • funny • helpful • …
He's my favourite person because he listens to me.	understands me • listens to me • helps me • plays with me • …

b) Gallery walk *Hänge dein Poster an die Wand. Sieh dir andere Poster an.*

My hero, your hero

1 Listening **Lily's neighbour**

a) Before you listen *Lily ist in der Wohnung ihres Nachbars Li-Jun. Sieh dir das Bild an und lies die Sätze. Umkreise die richtige Antwort: A oder B?*

1 Lily and Li-Jun are	A drinking tea.	B playing video games.
2 Li-June is	A on TV.	B in the newspaper.

b) **Listen.** (Circle) **the right answers.** *Höre zu. Umkreise die richtigen Antworten.*

1 Li-Jun saved[1] a little boy at the	A pool.	B beach.
2 The boy went into the water[2] to get his	A car.	B football.

c) **Match Lily's questions and Li-Jun's answers. Draw lines. Then listen and check.**
Ordne Lilys Fragen Li-Juns Antworten zu. Ziehe Linien. Höre zu und überprüfe.

1 Did you help somebody?	a No, he didn't.
2 Did the boy go underwater[3]?	b Yes, I did.
3 Did the boy get hurt[4]?	c Two days ago[5].
4 When did it happen?	d Yes, he did.

2 Looking at language **The simple past: *yes/no*-questions and short answers**
Sieh dir die Fragen und Antworten an. Ergänze die Regeln in der Box.

Erklär-film

Did you *help* somebody? – *Yes*, I *did*.   *Did* he *get* hurt? – *No*, he *didn't*.

Fragen im *simple past* fangen meistens mit _____ an.
Das Verb (*help, go, do, ...*) folgt dann in der Grundform.

Als **Kurzantwort** sagst du: *Yes, I* _____ oder *No, I* _____.

▶ Extra practice 2, p. 65

---

[1] **save** *retten*   [2] **water** *Wasser*   [3] **underwater** *unter Wasser*   [4] **get hurt** *sich verletzen*
[5] **two days ago** *vor zwei Tagen*

3 Speaking About Li-Jun

a) *Partner/in B: Gehe zur Seite 64.*
Partner/in A: Ergänze die Kurzantworten. Beantworte dann mit diesen Kurzantworten die Fragen von Partner/in B.

1 Yes, he *did*____. 2 No, he _____. 3 No, he _____. 4 Yes, he _____.

b) *Stelle Partner/in B diese Fragen. Schreibe Y für „yes" und N für „no".*

1 Did Li-Jun get married? ☐   3 Did he always live on Whitehawk Estate? ☐

2 Did he have a son? ☐   4 Did he stop work a long time ago? ☐

4 When you were five years old

a) **Complete the questions with *did*.** *Ergänze die Fragen mit* did.

1 _____ your family have a pet?   3 _____ you have a big bedroom?

2 _____ you like football?   4 _____ your grandparents live near you?

b) **Ask the questions 1–4. Answer them. Say *"Yes, I did"* or *"No, I didn't".***
Stelle die Fragen 1–4. Beantworte sie. Sage „Yes, I did" oder „No, I didn't".

▶ Extra practice 3–4, p. 66

5 Looking at language The simple past: questions with question words

Erklär-film

Sieh dir die zwei Fragen an. Ergänze die Regel.

1 When did it happen?

2 What did Lily ask Li-Jun?

Wenn am Anfang der Frage ein Fragewort (z.B. *when*) steht, folgt danach _____.

6 Lily's school day

Ergänze Li-Juns Fragen.
Nutze die Wörter aus der Box.

| how • where • why |

1 _____ did you come back late? – I had a problem with my bike.

2 _____ did you get home? – I took the bus.

3 _____ did you put your bike? – It's at school.

▶ Extra practice 5–6, p. 67

7 Listening **Our heroes**

a) Before you listen *Welche Menschen sind für dich Heldinnen oder Helden? Sprecht miteinander. Nutzt auch die Begriffe aus der Box.*

b) Listen and match the teenagers with their heroes. Draw lines.
Höre zu und ordne die Teenager ihren Helden / Heldinnen zu. Ziehe Linien.

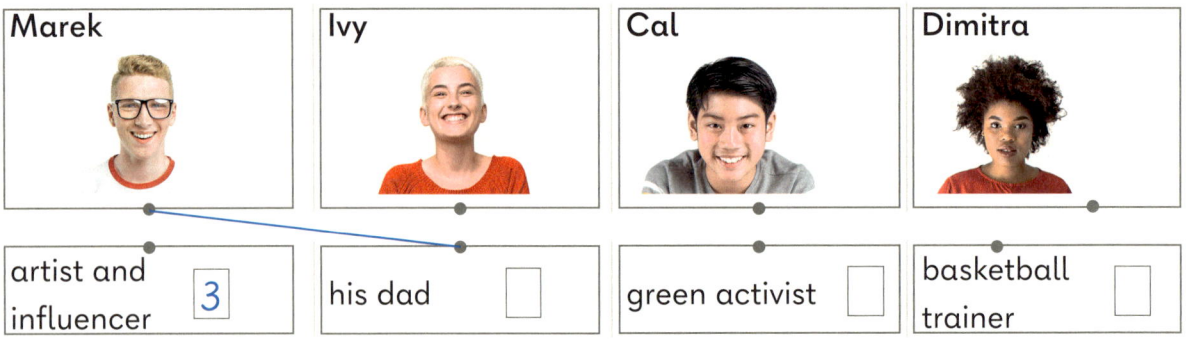

Marek	Ivy	Cal	Dimitra

| artist and influencer **3** | his dad ☐ | green activist ☐ | basketball trainer ☐ |

c) Listen again. Read the sentences. Write numbers 1–4 next to the right hero in b).
Höre noch einmal zu. Lies die Sätze. Schreibe die Nummern 1–4 neben den richtigen Helden / die richtige Heldin in b).

This hero ...

1 doesn't have favourites in the team.
2 wants to help our planet.
3 gives money to animal charities[3].
4 works long hours and helps many people.

8 Words **Opposites**

a) Word building *Lies die Box rechts. Was sind die Gegenteile der Wörter 1–4? Schreibe un davor.*

1 *un* cool   3 ____ happy

2 ____ friendly   4 ____ tidy

b) *Wir können nicht immer Gegensätze mit un- bilden. Ordne diese Gegensatzpaare einander zu. Ziehe Linien.*

1	good		a	wrong
2	right		b	horrible
3	nice		c	bad

c) *Führt ein Wort von a) oder b) vor. Wechselt euch ab. Ratet, was vorgeführt wird.*

Wenn du *un-* an den Anfang eines Wortes schreibst, bedeutet es das Gegenteil.

friendly

unfriendly (= not friendly)

---

[1] **activist** *Aktivist, Aktivistin*   [2] **artist** *Künstler, Künstlerin*   [3] **charity** *wohltätige Organisation*

9 Speaking Two student heroes

a) *Partner/in B: Gehe auf Seite 64.*
Partner/in A: Lies über Destiny.
Beantworte die Fragen von Partner/in B.

b) *Stelle Partner/in B Fragen über Jonah.*

1 Why did Jonah stay[3] in hospital for a long time?
2 What did people say about Jonah?
3 What did Jonah want to do?
4 How did he do this?

Destiny

1 Destiny's football team needed money for new sports clothes.
2 She skateboarded for ten kilometres[1] in a superhero costume[2]!
3 Her parents, friends and people on the street gave her money.
4 Her team was very happy with their new football clothes!

My task

10 My hero

▶ Digital help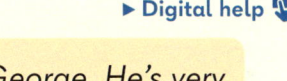

Schreibe über deine Heldin oder deinen Helden.
Er/Sie kann ein Familienmitglied sein, ein Freund / eine Freundin oder eine berühmte Person. Du kannst die Ideen in den Boxen nutzen.

My hero is George. He's very funny. He learned a bad word from Nish. He said it in front of Meera's friend!

My hero is (name) _____.

My hero is _____.

My hero _____
_____
_____
_____

| kind • funny • clever • brave • … |

| helped | me • many people • animals • the planet • … |

| had a great idea • worked hard • is good at … • … |

---

[1] **kilometre (km)** *Kilometer*   [2] **costume** *Kostüm, Verkleidung*   [3] **stay** *bleiben*

Digital quiz 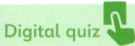 **Ich kann** Fragen über Helden und Heldinnen stellen und sie beantworten.

fifty-one **51**

Superheroes

1 Reading **Who is it?**

a) Before you read *Lily, Noah, Sunita und Zane haben ihre eigenen Superhelden und Superheldinnen gezeichnet. Kannst du erraten, wer welches Bild gezeichnet hat?*

Lily: A _____   Noah: _____   Sunita: _____   Zane: _____

b) *Bildet Gruppen aus vier Kindern. Jedes Kind liest einen Text auf Seite 53. Waren eure Antworten in a) richtig?*

Good to know

Du sagst die Jahreszahlen auf Englisch so:
1960: nineteen sixty   2006: two thousand and six   2021: twenty twenty-one

▶ Extra practice 7, p. 67

2 Words **Clothes**

a) *Lies den letzten Satz in jedem Superhelden-Text auf Seite 53 noch einmal. Beschrifte die Bilder in 1 mit den richtigen Wörtern. Nutze die Wörter in der Box.*

boots • cape • dress • helmet • mask • swimsuit • trousers

b) *Welches Kostüm gefällt dir in 1 am besten? Umkreise den passenden Buchstaben.*

I like A / B / C / D best.

▶ Extra practice 8, p. 68

c) *Zeichne Bilder zu einzelnen Kleidungsstücken.*

▶ Wordbank 3, p. 162

1 My name is ComputerGirl. I was born in 2006 on Planet Voria. I'm very clever and I can get into computers. But I want to use my power to help people. I wear long black boots and a silver helmet.
Sunita

2 Dolphin[1] Man here! I was born in the sea in 2008. When people put chemicals[2] in the water in 2020, I became part person and part dolphin. I can swim very fast and stay in water for a long time. I wear a silver swimsuit.
Zane

3 I'm Superdog. I was born on earth in 2002. But in 2019 when I ate some dog food for a dare[3], I became a dog! I have very strong teeth and a good nose. I wear a blue cape, blue trousers and a blue eye mask.
Noah

4 I'm The Climber. I can climb very fast! I was born in 1960 on planet Octo. Bad snakes travelled to our planet and killed my family, so I came to earth. I have eight arms to fight bad people. I wear a purple dress and a purple cape.
Lily

My task

3 Me as a superhero
▶ Digital help

a) *Schreibe in dein Heft über dich als Superheldin oder Superheld. Nutze die Tabelle mit den Ideen. Beginne mit:* My name is …

I wear	a helmet / an eye mask / a swimsuit / a dress / a cape / trousers / boots / …
I am	very brave / clever / fast / strong / …
I have	good eyes / a good nose / eight feet / …
I can	become an animal / do magic tricks / stop bad people / swim / talk to animals / fight / answer every question / …

▶ Wordbank 3–4, pp. 162–163

 b) *Stellt einander eure Texte vor.*

---

[1] **dolphin** *Delfin*   [2] **chemicals** *Chemikalien*   [3] **dare** *Mutprobe*

A great team!

1 Reading **An accident**

a) Before you read **Look at the pictures.** (Circle) **the right answers in blue.**
Sieh dir die Bilder an. Umkreise die richtigen Antworten in Blau.

1 The kids[1] were at (Lily's estate) / school.
2 Lily showed[2] the kids how to make pizza / do parkour.
3 Then I think Lily / Finn had an accident[3].

b) **Read the story. Then** (circle) **the correct summary: A or B?**
Lies die Geschichte. Umkreise dann die richtige Zusammenfassung: A oder B?

A The friends helped Finn after he fell. He needed to go to hospital.
B Finn had an accident. The friends didn't know what to do.

Last Saturday the four friends and Finn were at Lily's estate. They were bored[4]. Finn asked about the friends' free time activities.

5 **Finn** What about you, Lily? What do you do in your free time?

Lily I do parkour. Do you know what that is?

Finn It's the same word in German, but 10 I don't know what people do.

Lily Look, let me show you.

Lily I can walk on the wall like this. Then I can jump down ... and land[5] on my feet like this!

15 **Finn** Wow, that was cool, Lily. I'm surprised how easy it looks. Let me try ...

Lily No, Finn! It looks easy, but it isn't.

But Finn didn't listen ...

---

[1] **kid** *Kind, Jugendliche(r)* [2] **show** *zeigen* [3] **accident** *Unfall* [4] **bored** *gelangweilt* [5] **land** *landen*

20 **Lily**   Get down, Finn! It's dangerous¹.

Finn   No, it's OK. I'm really good at jumping!

Finn jumped ... and fell. The kids were really worried². Finn's face was very white.

25 **Lily**   Finn, are you OK?

Finn   My ankle hurts – and my head too.

Sunita   OK, let's call³ 999. ... Hello, I need an ambulance, please. Yes, my name's Sunita Chandra.

30   My friend Finn fell. His head and ankle hurt. ... Yes, Finn Demir, he's twelve. We're on Whitehawk Estate in Brighton ... Yes, thanks.

Sunita   Don't move⁴ your legs, Finn.

35   Stay warm, and please don't fall asleep!

Noah   We must⁵ stay calm.

Then Lily got a warm blanket.

Zane   I can talk to Finn, so he doesn't

40   fall asleep.

Zane told Finn some jokes and Finn tried to be brave. Sunita called Finn's mum.

Finn   Is the ambulance coming? I feel bad.

45 **Noah**   The ambulance is here. It's OK, Finn.

Man   Hello Finn, I need to check you out. Right ... and now let's get you in the ambulance!

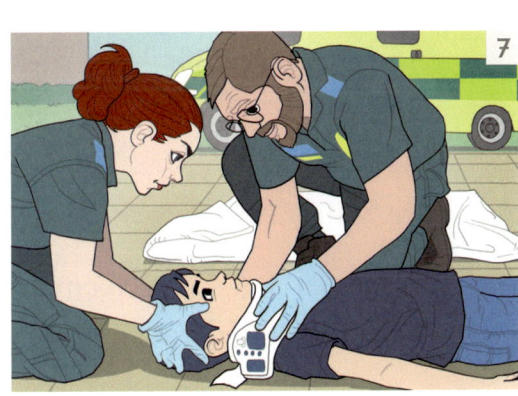

50 Then Finn's mum was there. She looked worried. She talked to Finn in the ambulance. Then Finn's mum and the four tired friends got in her car and went to the hospital.

---

¹ **dangerous** *gefährlich*   ² **be worried** *sich Sorgen machen*   ³ **call** *anrufen*   ⁴ **move** *bewegen*
⁵ **must** *müssen*

2   What did they do?

Who did what? Write Finn, Lily, Sunita or Zane. *Wer hat was getan? Schreibe Finn, Lily, Sunita oder Zane.*

Good to know

In Großbritannien wählst du 999 für einen Krankenwagen, die Feuerwehr oder die Polizei.

1 _____ called 999 and Finn's mum.

2 _____ got a warm blanket.

3 _____ told funny stories.

4 _____ tried to be brave.

3   Words **Parts of the body**

Write the words under the pictures.
Schreibe die Wörter unter die Bilder.

ankle • arm • head • ~~face~~ • feet • leg

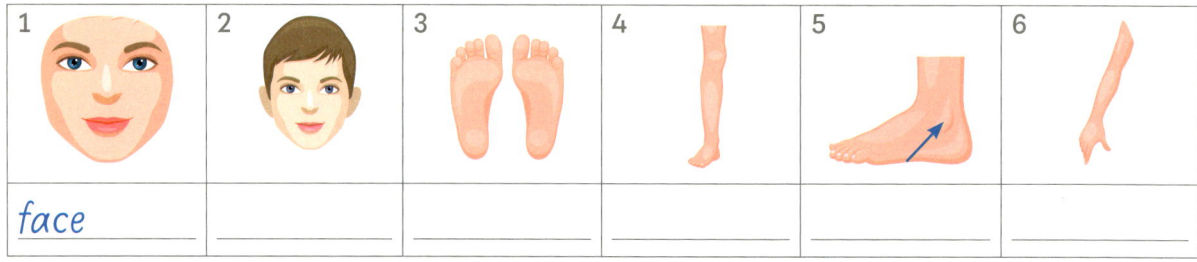

1	2	3	4	5	6
face	_____	_____	_____	_____	_____

▶ Wordbank 4, p. 163   ▶ Extra practice 9, p. 68

4   Listening **The end of the story**

Die Kinder sind im Wartezimmer des Krankenhauses. Sind diese Sätze richtig (✓) oder falsch (✕)? Höre zu.

1 Finn's head hurts very much.		3 He wants to see his friends.	
2 Finn feels fine.		4 Finn thought Zane's jokes were funny.	

5   Life Skills **Teamwork**

Die Kinder in der Geschichte haben im Team gearbeitet. Wann arbeitest du im Team? Erzähle darüber.

I work in a team when I ...

do sports. • am with my friends. • am at school. • am with my family.

Digital quiz   **Ich kann** eine Geschichte über Teamarbeit verstehen.

Brighton stories: Special people

1 A present for Gloria's uncle

Before you watch *Glorias Lieblingsonkel heiratet. Was könnte Gloria ihm und seiner neuen Frau schenken? Hake (✓) ein Bild ab oder mehrere.*

1	2	3	4	5
a photo	an umbrella	a book	a video	a ticket for a show

2 Viewing Gloria's present

a) Watch the first part. Read the questions and (circle) the correct answers.
Sieh dir den ersten Teil an. Lies die Fragen und umkreise die richtigen Antworten.

1 What's Joe's idea?   A Chocolates   B A video   C A photo
2 Does Gloria like Joe's idea?   A Yes   B No

b) Watch the second part. Match the kids to their roles. Draw lines.
Sieh dir den zweiten Teil an. Ordne die Kinder ihren Rollen zu. Ziehe Linien.

Joe
Daisy
Emir
Gloria

A plays the girlfriend.
B plays the uncle.
C films the video.
D holds the props[1].

3 Now you

Read the questions. (Circle) **Yes** or **No.** *Lies die Fragen. Umkreise „Yes" oder „No".*

Do Uncle Tim and Aunt Claire like the present?	Yes	No
Do you like the present?	Yes	No

---

[1] **hold the props** *die Requisiten halten*

Work out meaning

1 Word building **Use word families**

Bildet Wortfamilien. Schreibt die blauen Wörter aus den Sätzen 1–3 an die richtigen Stellen in der Tabelle. Was bedeuten die Wörter auf Deutsch?

1 Finn showed great bravery when he had the accident.
2 Finn plays games online. He's often the winner.
3 Happiness for Finn is a computer and his cat!

happy	*happiness*
glücklich	*Glück*
brave	_____
mutig	_____
win	_____
gewinnen	_____

2 Use German and other languages

a) *Finn spricht Deutsch, Türkisch und Englisch. Er versteht viele englische Wörter, weil sie wie im Deutschen sind:*
Englisch: *arm* — Deutsch: *Arm*

Manche Wörter sehen in unterschiedlichen Sprachen ähnlich aus und haben die gleiche Bedeutung.

Manche englischen Wörter sind nicht wie im Deutschen, aber wie im Türkischen:
Englisch: *ambulance* – Deutsch: *Krankenwagen* — Türkisch: *ambulans*

Ordnet die blauen Wörter den deutschen Wörtern zu. Zieht Linien.

1 Finn has a German and a Turkish passport.	a Würmer
2 Finn loves to buy cakes from the bakery.	b Pass
3 Finn's favourite sea animals are whales.	c Bäckerei
4 He doesn't like worms!	d Wale

b) *Manche englischen Wörter sehen wie deutsche Wörter aus, aber sie haben eine andere Bedeutung. Wähle das richtige englische Wort aus der Box.*

get • good

False friends
sehen in unterschiedlichen Sprachen ähnlich aus, haben aber verschiedene Bedeutungen, z. B. *become* und *brave*.

1 I ~~become~~ _____ money from my dad every week.

2 Buddy is a ~~brave~~ _____ dog. He always listens to Noah.

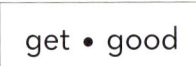 Digital quiz **Ich kann** die Bedeutung neuer Wörter ableiten. ✓

Make a quiz about heroes

Step 1

Du wirst ein Quiz über Heldinnen und Helden machen. Lies zuerst über den Profiboxer Muhammad Ali.

Muhammad Ali

– was born in 1942 in the USA
– died[1] in 2016
– was a boxer
– fought against[2] racism[3]

Step 2

Lies die Fragen über Muhammad Ali und beantworte sie im simple past.

When was Muhammad Ali born?	*He was born in* _____
When did he die?	_____
What did he do?	_____ _____ _____

Step 3

Lies über die Widerstandskämpferin Sophie Scholl. Schreibe drei Fragen über sie in dein Heft. Schreibe die Antworten dazu. Nutze das simple past.

Sophie Scholl

– was born in 1921 in Germany
– died in 1943
– was a student
– fought against Nazi Germany

Step 4

Mache das Quiz mit einer Person in deiner Klasse. Beantworte die Fragen dieser Person und stelle ihr deine Fragen.

---

[1] **die** *(simple past: died) sterben*   [2] **against** *gegen*   [3] **racism** *Rassismus*

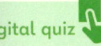 Ich kann Informationen recherchieren und ein Quiz machen.

1 Speaking **Who is it?**

a) **Describe a Varndean kid.**
Beschreibe ein Varndean Kind.

hair braces tie eyes glasses

This kid has _____

Noah

Sunita

Zane

Faye

Lily

Jodie

Mihai

Sophia

This kid has long, black hair.

 b) **Read your sentences. Guess who the others described.**
Lies deine Sätze vor. Rate, wen die anderen beschrieben haben.

That's Sunita!

2 Listening **A group project**

a) *Noah, Sunita, Lily und Zane müssen eine Präsentation über die Geschichte von Brighton halten. Höre zu. Lies dann die Sätze. Umkreise die richtigen Eigenschaften der Kinder.*

1 Noah has a lot of notes from the lessons.
He is   A hard-working.   B confident.

2 Sunita is good with computers.
She is   A kind.   B clever.

3 Lily can help Noah.
She's   A kind.   B hard-working.

4 Zane can present it.
He is   A clever.   B confident.

b) **Listen again and check.** *Höre noch einmal zu und überprüfe.*

Check

3 Language **Sports heroes**

a) Read Lily's message to her friends. Then write their questions in the *simple past*.
Lies Lilys Nachricht. Schreibe dann die Fragen ihrer Freunde und Freundinnen im simple past.

Yesterday I saw my parkour hero Lexie Gallagher. She's the best in England!

1 ... see her / in Brighton? / you

Did you _____

2 ... you / have / a good time?

_____

3 ... to her / you / talk?

_____

4 ... you / do / some parkour with her?

_____

b) Now complete Lily's short answers to the questions in **a)**.
Ergänze jetzt Lilys Kurzantworten zu den Fragen in a).

1 Yes, *I did* ___. 2 Yes, _____. 3 Yes, _____. 4 No, _____.

c) Read Zane's message. (Circle) the correct question word.
Lies Zanes Nachricht. Umkreise das richtige Fragewort.

Read the answers! They can help you.

I saw my heroes too – Albion FC!

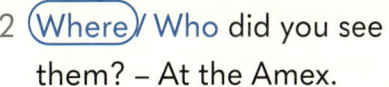

1 (When)/ How did you see them? – On Saturday afternoon.
2 (Where)/ Who did you see them? – At the Amex.
3 (How)/ What did they play? – They were great.
4 (Who)/ Why did you watch the game with? – With Holly.
5 How /(What) did you do after the game? – I went swimming.

VARNDEAN Teen Zine

Topics: Friends and heroes

*Our **top ten list** of the things that we like to do with our friends!*

What do you like to do with your friends? Write your numbers 1–10 in the boxes.

1. have a sleepover[1]

2. listen to music

3. have a picnic

4. chat online

5. play video games

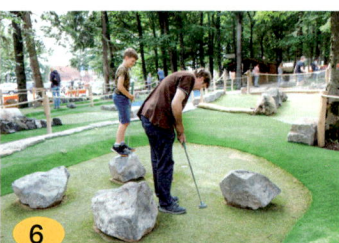

6. play mini golf

7. look at videos on our phones

8. play cards

9. tell each other[2] jokes

10. watch films

Send us your top ten lists!

---

[1] **sleepover** *Übernachtungsparty*   [2] **each other** *einander*

Heroes

October is Black History Month! Here are two of our favourite Black heroes. Do you know more?

Lewis Hamilton
Formula 1 driver

Lewis Hamilton was born in the UK in 1985. He is one of the best drivers of all time!
But people are racist[1] – they treat[2] him badly. Lewis says it is time for white people to stop this!

Doreen Lawrence
anti-racist activist

Doreen Lawrence came to the UK from Jamaica when she was a little girl. In 1993 Doreen's son Stephen was killed in a racist attack when he was 18 years old. Doreen has worked very hard for fairness for her son and other Black people.

E-postcard from the USA

Lea from Varndean is on a school exchange[3] in the USA.

Hi from San Francisco!

The school exchange[3] is great! It's easy to make friends here because there are a lot of clubs: dance, parkour, cooking, computers ... and lots more!

One of my best friends is Luisa. She was born in the USA, but her parents are from Mexico. They speak[4] Spanish at home and now Luisa is teaching me some Spanish.

Have a good day!

Lea

¡Hola!

---

[1] **racist** *rassistisch*   [2] **treat** *behandeln*   [3] **exchange** *Austauchprogramm*   [4] **speak** *sprechen*

Partner page

👥 **3** Speaking **About Li-Jun** ▶ Page 49

a) *Partner/in B: Stelle Partner/in A diese Fragen. Schreibe Y für „yes" und N für „no".*

1 Did Li-Jun live in China? ☐

2 Did he want to leave[1] China? ☐

3 Did he always live in Brighton? ☐

4 Did he get a job in the UK[2]? ☐

b) *Partner/in B: Ergänze die Kurzantworten. Beantworte dann mit diesen Kurzantworten die Fragen von Partner/in A.*

1 Yes, he *did*____.   2 No, he _____.   3 No, he _____.   4 Yes, he _____.

👥 **9** Speaking **Two student heroes** ▶ Page 51

a) *Partner/in B: Stetelle Partner/in A Fragen zu Destiny.*

1 Why did Destiny need money?
2 What did she do?
3 Who did she get money from?
4 How did her team feel?

b) *Partner/in B: Lies über Jonah. Beantworte die Fragen von Partner/in A.*

1 Jonah stayed in hospital for a long time because he was very ill[3].
2 People said he was always kind to everybody.

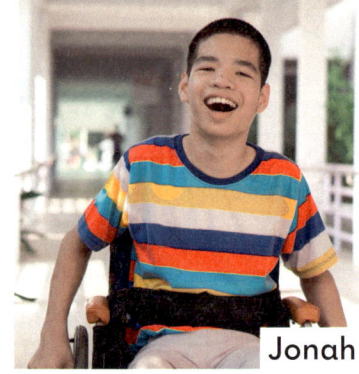
Jonah

3 Jonah wanted to say thank you to everybody when he left[1] the hospital.
4 So he did a magic show in the hospital.

---

¹ **leave,** *simple past:* **left** *verlassen*   ² **UK (=United Kingdom)** *Vereinigtes Königreich*   ³ **ill** *krank*

Extra practice

▶ page 44

Extra practice 1

a) **Write about someone in your class or at school. You can use the words in the box.**
Schreibe über jemanden in deiner Klasse oder Schule. Du kannst die Wörter in der Box nutzen.

brave • clever • confident • good at sports • good with computers • hard-working • nice

blond • black • brown • red • curly • long • short • straight

My person has _____ hair and _____ .

My person is _____ and _____ .

b) Read your sentences **Take turns and guess. Who is the person?**
Lies deine Sätze vor. Wechselt euch ab und ratet. Wer ist die Person?

My person has red curly hair and brown eyes.
My person is clever and hard-working.

Is it Eliana?

▶ page 48

Extra practice 2

Read the questions and circle the correct short answer.
Lies die Fragen und umkreise die richtigen Kurzantworten.

1 Did you eat lunch two days ago?   A Yes, I did.   B Yes, he did.

2 Did your grandparents live in London?   A No, it didn't.   B No, they didn't.

3 Did he go to the park?   A Yes, he did.   B Yes, you did.

4 Did they eat all the cake?   A No, they didn't. B No, we didn't.

5 Did your class have a party?   A Yes, he did.   B Yes, it did.

6 Did she see the film?   A No, she didn't. B No, you didn't.

▶ page 49

Extra practice 3

Lily is asking Noah about Buddy. Complete the conversation with *did*.

Lily fragt Noah über Buddy. Ergänze das Gespräch mit did.

Lily   _Did you get_   (1 you / get) Buddy
when he was small?

Noah   No, we didn't. He was a year old.

Lily   _____ (2 he / come) from
another home?

Noah   No, he didn't. He had training.

Lily   _____ (3 he / learn) to be
so good and quiet?

Noah   Yes, he did. He's never scared or mean.

Lily   _____ (4 you / love) Buddy?

Noah   Yes, I did. He's so cute and friendly!

Lily   _____ (5 your parents / help) you look after
him?

Noah   Yes, they did at first. But now I look after him.

▶ page 49

Extra practice 4

Nish spricht mit seiner Freundin Talia. Schreibe Talias Fragen.

Talia	Nish
1 the homework? / do / Did you	
Did you _____	No, I didn't.
2 go away / Did you / for the weekend?	
_____	Yes, I did.
3 in London? / visit friends / Did you	
_____	Yes, I did.
4 write me / a message? / Did you	
_____	No, I didn't.

Extra practice 5 ▶ page 49

Read the questions and answers. Circle the correct question words.

Lies die Fragen und Antworten. Umkreise das richtige Fragewort.

1 (What time) / who did you get up?   – At six o'clock.
2 How / What did you go to school?   – By bike.
3 Who / How did you see?   – A friend.
4 What / Where did you go after school?   – To my football training.
5 Who / What did you have for dinner?   – I had pasta.

Extra practice 6 ▶ page 49

Read the questions and answers. Circle the correct question word.

Lies die Fragen und Antworten. Umkreise das richtige Fragewort.

1 When / (Where) did you go after the football game?   – I went home.
2 Why / How did you go home?   – I was tired.
3 How / Where did you get home?   – I took the bus with a friend.
4 When / Who did you take the bus with?   – My friend Erica.
5 How / What did you do at home?   – I watched videos.
6 When / Where did you go to bed?   – Too late! At 11 o'clock.

Extra practice 7 ▶ page 52

a) **Say the dates. Take turns.** *Sagt die Daten. Wechselt euch ab.*

1 the sixth of June   4 the third of July
2 the eleventh of September   5 the twenty-second of February
3 the twentieth of May   6 the twenty-first of March

My favourite day is the first of April. That's my birthday!

b) **Now say the years. Take turns.**

Sagt jetzt die Jahreszahlen. Wechselt euch ab.

1 twenty twenty-two   4 eighteen ninety-five
2 nineteen sixty-eight   5 nineteen ninety-nine
3 seventeen fifty   6 two thousand and nine

Extra practice 8 ▶ page 52

What are they wearing? Use the words in the box.

Was haben sie an? Nutze die Wörter in der Box.

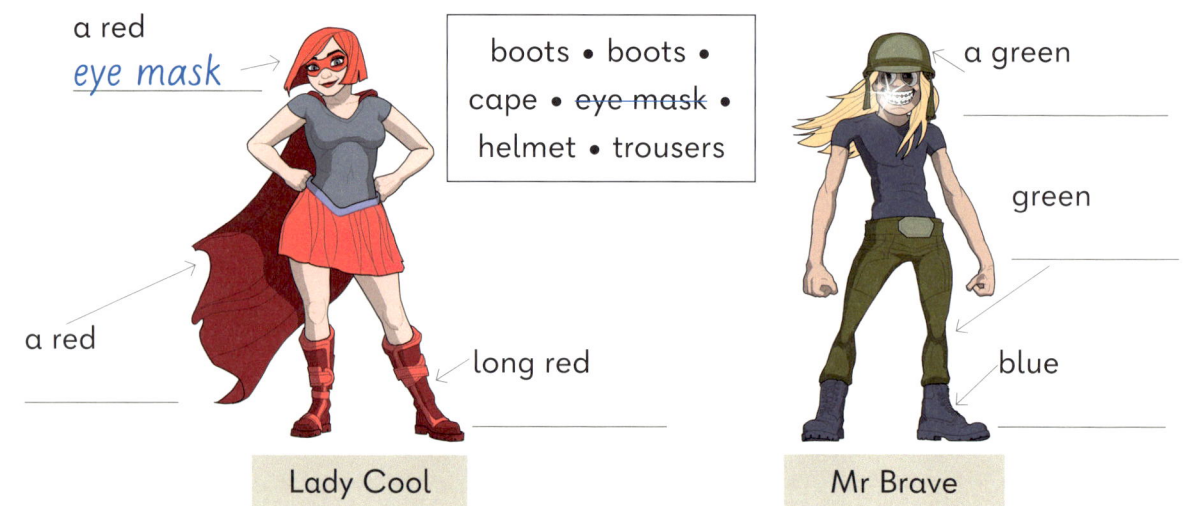

a red
eye mask

boots • boots •
cape • ~~eye mask~~ •
helmet • trousers

a red

long red

Lady Cool

a green

green

blue

Mr Brave

Extra practice 9 ▶ page 56

Match the parts of the body with the correct photos. Draw lines.

Ordne die Körperteile den richtigen Fotos zu. Ziehe Linien.

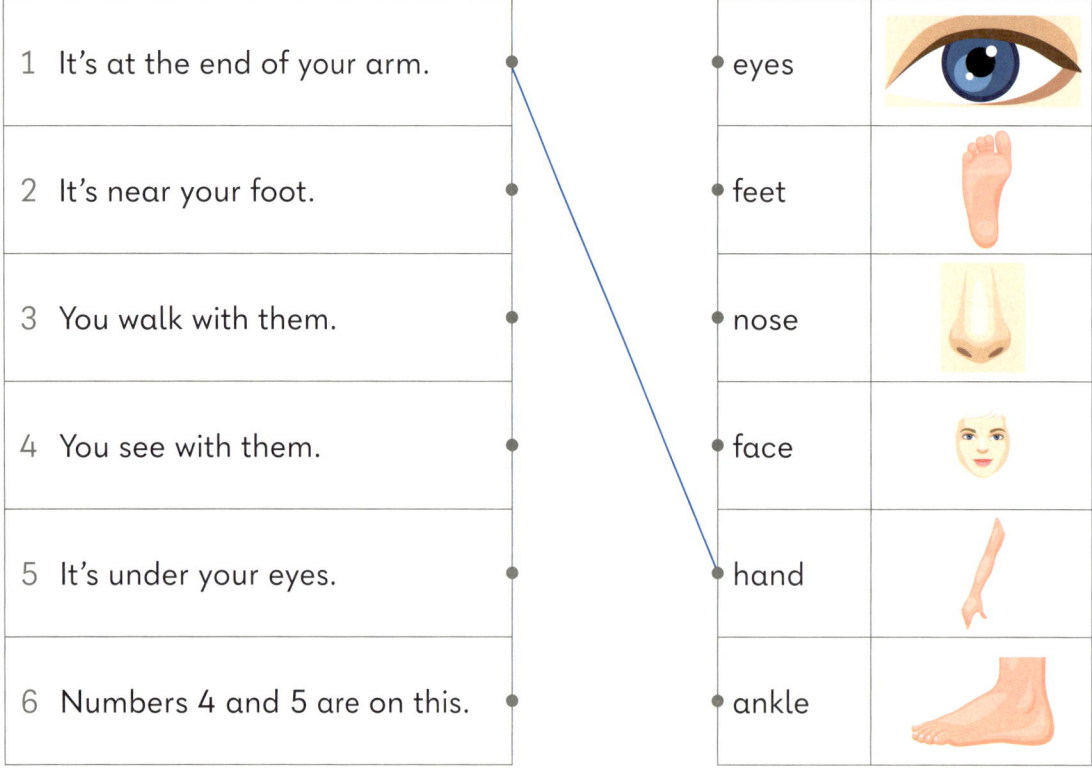

1 It's at the end of your arm.	eyes
2 It's near your foot.	feet
3 You walk with them.	nose
4 You see with them.	face
5 It's under your eyes.	hand
6 Numbers 4 and 5 are on this.	ankle

Unit 2

Friends and heroes

▶ p. 42	**eye**	das Auge	an **eye**
	curly	lockig	
	hair	das Haar, die Haare	
	glasses *(pl)*	die Brille	braces — glasses
	straight	gerade; *(Haare)* glatt	
	braces *(pl)*	die Zahnspange, die Zahnklammer	
▶ p. 43	**person**	die Person	

Topic 1

▶ p. 44	**kind**	nett, freundlich
	hard-working	fleißig
	confident	(selbst)sicher; zuversichtlich
	(to) **be good at** sth.	etwas gut können; gut in etwas sein
	brave	mutig
	like her	wie sie
	tall	groß *(Person)*; hoch *(Gebäude)*
	helpful	hilfsbereit; hilfreich, nützlich
▶ p. 46	(to) **think of** sb./sth.	an jemanden/etwas denken

Topic 2

▶ p. 48	**newspaper**	die Zeitung
▶ p. 50	**hero,** *pl* **heroes**	der Held, die Heldin
	planet	der Planet

▶ p. 51   **superhero,** *Mehrzahl* **superheroes**   der Superheld, die Superheldin

    (to) **give: they gave**   geben: sie gaben, sie haben gegeben

    (to) **stay**   bleiben

    (to) **learn**   lernen

    word   das Wort

Topic 3

▶ p. 52   **thousand**   tausend

    boot   der Stiefel

    dress   das Kleid

    helmet   der Helm

    mask   die Maske

    swimsuit   der Badeanzug

    trousers *(pl)*   die Hose

boots

helmets

▶ p. 53   I was **born**   ich wurde geboren

    power   die Kraft, die Macht

    (to) **become,** *simple past:* **became**   werden

    part … part …   teils … teils …

    strong   stark

    nose   die Nase

    (to) **climb**   klettern (auf)

    (to) **kill**   töten

    earth   die Erde

    (to) **fight,** *simple past:* **fought**   kämpfen; bekämpfen

    foot, *pl* **feet**   der Fuß

Story

▶ p. 54   (to) **show**   zeigen

    accident   der Unfall

    (to) **fall,** *simple past:* **fell**   fallen; hinfallen

    German   deutsch; Deutsch; der/die Deutsche

    wall   die Wand, die Mauer

(to) **jump**	springen	
like this	so, auf diese Art	
down	hinunter, herunter	
easy	einfach, leicht	
(to) **look**	aussehen	
(to) listen	zuhören	
▶p.55 **face**	das Gesicht	my **ankle** hurts.
ankle	der Knöchel, das Fußgelenk	
(to) **hurt**, *simple past:* **hurt**	schmerzen, wehtun	
head	der Kopf	
ambulance	der Krankenwagen	an **ambulance**
leg	das Bein	
(to) **fall asleep**	einschlafen	
can	können	
blanket	die Decke *(zum Zudecken)*	
joke	der Witz, der Scherz	
(to) **need to do** sth.	etwas tun müssen	
(to) **check** sb. **out**	jemanden untersuchen	
▶p.56 **arm**	der Arm	

Study skills

▶p.58 **Turkish**	türkisch; Türkisch

Unit 3
Activities and games

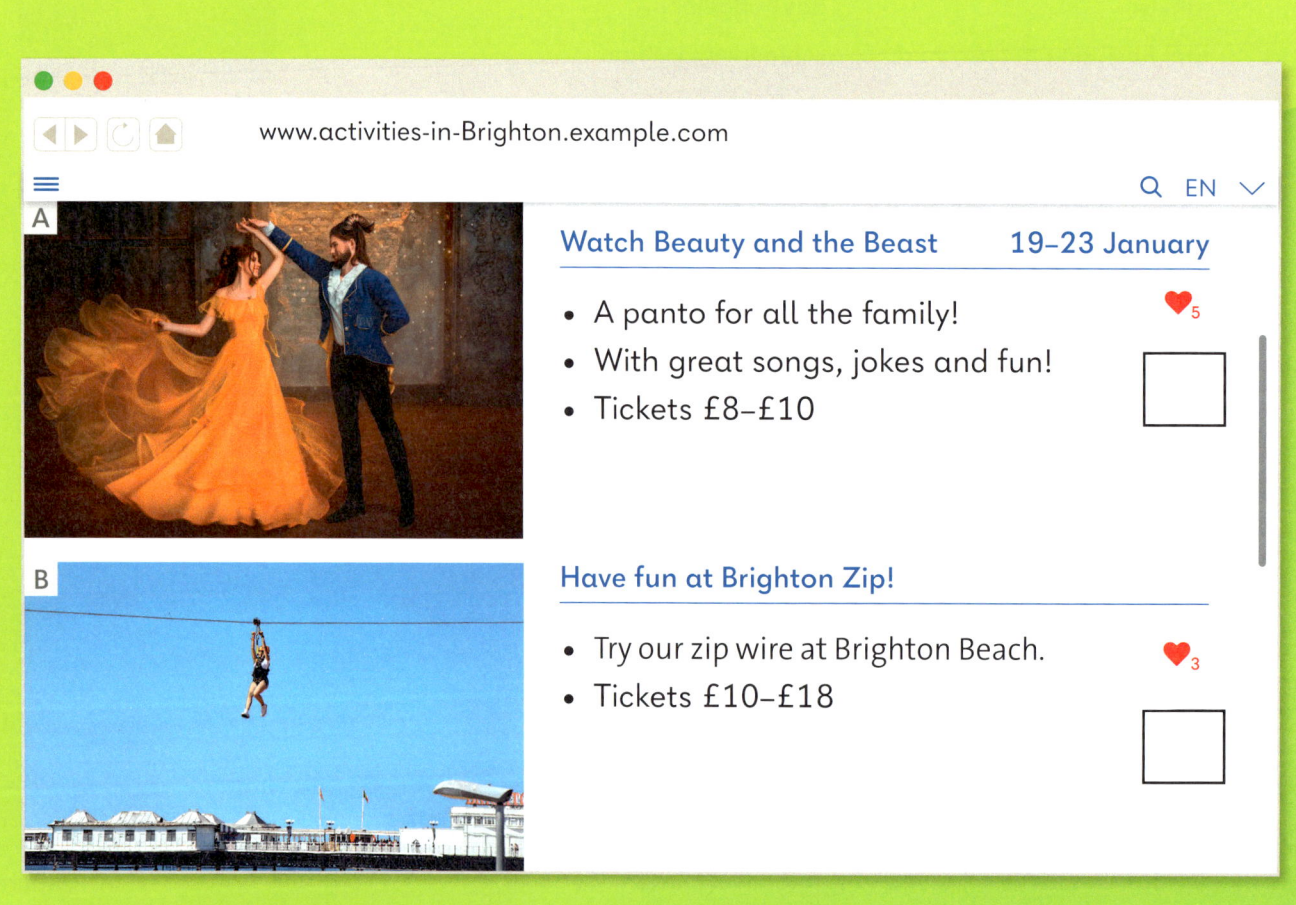

www.activities-in-Brighton.example.com

A

Watch Beauty and the Beast   **19–23 January**

- A panto for all the family!
- With great songs, jokes and fun!
- Tickets £8–£10

♥ 5

B

Have fun at Brighton Zip!

- Try our zip wire at Brighton Beach.
- Tickets £10–£18

♥ 3

1   Listening   **What's on in Brighton**

a)   Before you listen   *Sieh dir die vier Aktivitäten in Brighton an. Welche magst du? Kreise sie ein und rede dann darüber.*

I think activity A / B / C / D looks interesting / cool / fun.

b)   **What does Zane's family want to do? Listen and tick (✓) the right activity.**
Was möchte Zanes Familie unternehmen? Höre zu und hake oben die richtige Aktivität ab.

Good to know

In Großbritannien ist eine *panto* (kurz für *pantomime*) ein lustiges Musical.

Nach dieser Unit kann ich ...

○ über Aktivitäten und Uhrzeiten sprechen
○ Pläne machen und darüber sprechen
○ Musik, Shows, Filme und Spiele vergleichen
○ einen Weg beschreiben
○ darüber sprechen, wie lange ich online bin
○ meine Meinung äußern

Unit task ✓

○ Aktivitäten für einen besonderen Tag an der Schule planen und vorstellen

www.activities-in-Brighton.example.com

Q EN ∨

C

Learn to cook Thai food!   **19 January**

• Cook great food!
• £40

♥2

D

Make your insect hotel!

• See lots of insects!
• A fun family activity
• It's free.

♥0

2 Listening **Booking tickets online**

a) *Zanes Mutter kauft Karten für eine Show. Wann müssen sie dort sein? Lies den Tipp und verbinde die Uhrzeiten.*

So kannst du die Uhrzeiten sagen:
1.45 = quarter to two
2.15 = quarter past two
2.30 = half past two

1	The first show starts at half past two.		2.15	
2	They have to get the tickets at quarter to two.		2.30	
3	They have to be in their seats at quarter past two.		1.45	

b) *Höre zu. Mache ein Häkchen in 2a) neben der Uhrzeit, an der die Show beginnt.*

▶ Extra practice 1–3, pp. 92–93

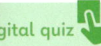 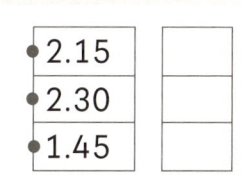

What are your plans?

1 Reading **School activity week in year 8**

a) Before you read *Im nächsten Monat ist Projektwoche. Sieh dir die Namen und Fotos der Aktivitäten an. Mache ein (✓) bei den Aktivitäten, die du kennst.*

Activity week – a week of fun!

4 Knitting
In this activity you can create a toy animal or a blanket at school.

1 Dungeons[1] and Dragons
Play this great game at school.

5 Karate
Do karate training with a trainer in Varndean's sports hall.

2 Goats and other animals
We are going to meet our school goats and other animals!

6 Tea party and show
Plan a summer tea party and show at Varndean. Sing and act in the show!

3 History in Brighton
Learn about Brighton's history. Visit Brighton Pavilion and Lewes Castle!

7 Photography
Learn about photography. Take photos at school and of street art in Brighton.

b) **Read about the activities. Write the numbers.**
Lies über die Aktivitäten. Schreibe die Nummern auf.

Which activity is good if you …

1 want to create something? **4**   2 like sports? ☐   3 like street art? ☐

4 like old buildings in Brighton? ☐   5 like games? ☐   6 like animals? ☐

7 like to sing? ☐

---

[1] **dungeon** *Kerker, Verlies*

2 Listening **What are you going to choose?**

a) Before you listen **Which of the activities in 1a) is the best one for the kids? Write the numbers. Then tell each other.** *Welche der Aktivitäten in 1a) sind die besten für die Kinder? Schreibe die Nummern auf. Erzählt es einander.*

I think the best activity for ...

A Lily is _____.   B Zane is _____.   C Noah is _____.   D Sunita is _____.

b) **Listen and draw lines.** *Höre zu und ziehe Linien.*

1 Lily: I'm going to choose	a Dungeons and Dragons.
2 Noah: I'm going to choose	b knitting.
3 Zane: I'm going to choose	c photography.
4 Sunita: I'm going to choose	d the tea party and show.

c) **Listen and draw lines again.** *Höre zu und ziehe Linien.*

1 Lily: I'm not going to choose	a goats and other animals.
2 Noah: I'm not going to choose	b karate.
3 Zane: I'm not going to choose	c photography.
4 Sunita: I'm not going to choose	d history in Brighton.

d) **What about you?** *Und du?*

I'm going to choose _____.

I'm not going to choose _____.

e) **Walk around** **Tell each other your top activity and what you aren't going to do.**
Erzählt einander eure Lieblingsaktivität und was ihr nicht tun werdet.

I'm going to choose karate. I'm not going to choose the tea party and show.

I'm going to choose the tea party and show.

Erklär-
film

3 Looking at language **The going to-future**

a) **Read the conversation.** *Lies das Gespräch.*

Lily _____ Yay, it's Friday! Do you have any plans for the weekend?

Zane _____ Yes, I'm going to help my dad at the cafe. What about you?

Lily _____ I'm not going to do anything special this evening. Tomorrow mum is going to make a cake and we're going to have a nice day.

b) **Draw lines.** *Ziehe Linien.*

1 Zane: I'm going to help	a a cake.
2 Lily's mum is going to make	b my dad at the cafe.
3 Lily and her mum are going to have	c a nice day.

c) (Circle) the right answer: **A** or **B**. *Umkreise die richtige Antwort: A oder B.*

Mit dem **going to-Futur** sprechen wir über …

A Pläne für die Zukunft (*tomorrow, next year*).

B die Vergangenheit (*yesterday, last year*).

Wir bilden das *going-to*-Futur mit einer Form von *be* + *going to* + Verb.

4 Zane's weekend

Complete Zane's plans and his family's plans with *'m, 's, 're*.
Ergänze Zanes Pläne und die Pläne seiner Familie mit 'm, 's, 're.

1 Holly is busy. On Saturday she___ going to play with a friend.

2 Mum and dad have plans. They___ going to have dinner in town.

3 On Sunday I___ going to make lunch. Then we___ going to watch a panto.

5 Plans for the weekend

Und du? Ergänze die Sätze. Dann erzählt euch eure Wochenendpläne.

do homework • play on the computer • go cycling • watch a film • see my friends • …

On Saturday I'm going to _____.

On Sunday I'm going to _____.

▶ Extra practice 4, p. 94

6 Looking at language **The going to-future (yes/no-questions)**

a) *Lies das Gespräch und unterstreiche das erste Wort in jeder Frage.*

b) *Was ist richtig? Umkreise A, B oder C.*

Going to-Fragen beginnen mit einer Form von …

A be.   B have.   C do.

George __ Are you going to have a date¹ tomorrow?
Scout __ Yes, I am.
George __ Is your friend going to meet you here?
Scout __ No, he isn't.
George __ Am I going to meet him?
Scout __ Yes, you are.

7 More questions for Scout

Role-play *Ziehe Linien. Dann spielt das Gespräch vor.*

George
1 Are you going to buy a new hat?
2 Is your friend going to swim to the date?
3 Are you and your friend going to have fun?

Scout
a No, he isn't.
b Yes, we are!
c Yes, I am.

Extra practice 5–6, pp. 94–95

My task

8 Make plans for the weekend

Partner/in B: Sieh dir Seite 92 an.
Partner/in A: Sieh dir deinen Kalender an. Finde eine Zeit, an der du dich mit Partner/in B treffen kannst. Du beginnst.

Partner A __ Hi! What are you going to do on Saturday afternoon? Can we play football?
Partner B __ Sorry, I can't. I'm going to … What about Saturday morning?
Partner A __ Sorry, I can't. I'm going to … What about Sunday afternoon?
Partner B __ Good idea! Let's meet at …
Partner A __ Great! See you then!
Partner B __ OK, bye!

Saturday	
visit grandpa	11.00
Sunday	
go swimming with Charlie	10.45

---

¹ **date** *Verabredung, Date*

 **Ich kann** Pläne machen und darüber sprechen.

Music, films and shows

1 Listening **What kind of music do you like?**

a) Before you listen *Sieh dir die Musikrichtungen (a–f) an. Welche Wörter sehen aus wie Wörter aus anderen Sprachen, die du kennst? Redet miteinander.*

a rap ☐   d electro ☐

b rock 1   e acoustic ☐

c pop ☐   f classical ☐

Rap is the same in German.

That's right!

b) *Höre sechs Musikclips. In welcher Reihenfolge hörst du sie? Schreibe 1–6 in die Tabelle in* a).

c) *Höre dir das Gespräch an. Beantworte die Fragen zu Lily (L), Noah (N), Sunita (S) und Zane (Z).*

1 Who loves rock?   Z

2 Who doesn't like rock?   ☐

3 Who likes rap?   ☐

4 Who likes electro?   ☐

d) **Which kinds of music do you like or not like? Use the words in** a) **or your own ideas.**
Welche Arten von Musik magst du? Welche nicht? Nutze die Wörter in a) *oder deine eigenen Ideen.*

I like electro, but I don't like acoustic. What about you?

I agree. / I don't agree. I love pop music.

Erklär-
film

2 Looking at language **Comparatives**

a) **Read 1–3. Then match the words (adjectives) on the right. Draw lines.**
Lies 1–3. Ordne dann die Wörter (Adjektive) rechts einander zu. Ziehe Linien.

1 Classical music is slower than other kinds of music.

2 Rap is more interesting than pop.

3 Electro is faster than acoustic.

1 slow (langsam)	a faster (schneller)
2 interesting (interessant)	b slower (langsamer)
3 fast (schnell)	c more interesting (interessanter)

b) *Ergänze die Regel. Sieh dir auch die Ausnahmen an.*

Personen und Dinge kann man miteinander vergleichen.

Bei kurzen Adjektiven hängst du _____ ans Ende des Adjektivs:
slow – slower.

Bei langen Adjektiven setzt du _____ vor das Adjektiv:
interesting – more interesting.

Rap is better than electro.

Pop is worse than classical

Ausnahmen:
good – *better*   bad – *worse*

3 **Comparing music**

Complete the sentences.
Ergänze die Sätze.

better • cooler • faster • more interesting • quieter • ~~slower~~ • worse

1 Noah: Classical music is *slower* _____ (slow) than rock.

2 Zane: Pop is _____ (bad) than classical music.

3 Lily: Rap is _____ (cool) and _____ (interesting) than pop. And rap is _____ (good) than electro.

4 Sunita: Electro is _____ (fast) than acoustic.

▶ Extra practice 7–8, pp. 95–96

4 Reading **What do you want to watch?**

a) Before you read *Sieh dir die Filmposter unten an. Um welche Art von Filmen handelt es sich? Schreibe 1–3 neben den richtigen Film.*

1 an action film   2 a cartoon[1]   3 a science fiction film

A

This is the **funniest** and the **best** cartoon of the year!

B

Dex 3000 isn't the **cleverest** robot, but he is very kind.

C

It's the **most exciting** job ever – in the **worst** place on the planet.

b) **Read the reviews in a). Then (circle) the correct sentence.**
   Lies die Filmbeschreibungen in a). Umkreise dann die richtige Aussage.

1 The cartoon is funny.   2 The robot isn't kind.   3 Agent Green's job is boring.

Erklär-
film

5 Looking at language **Superlatives**

a) *Lies die Sätze 1–3. Ordne dann die Wörter einander zu. Ziehe Linien.*

1 This is the funniest cartoon of the year!   2 Dex 3000 isn't the cleverest robot.

3 It's the most exciting job ever!

1 funny (lustig)	a most exciting (am aufregendsten)
2 clever (schlau, klug)	b cleverest (am schlauesten)
3 exciting (aufregend)	c funniest (am lustigsten)

b) *Sieh dir a) an und ergänze die Regel. Lies auch die Ausnahmen.*

Wenn ich sagen möchte, was ich am lustigsten, am aufregendsten usw. finde,
hänge ich bei kurzen Adjektiven _____ ans Ende.
Bei langen Adjektiven setze ich _____ vor das Adjektiv.
Ausnahmen: *good – better – best*   *bad – worse – worst*

---

[1] **cartoon** *Zeichentrickfilm*

6 Speaking **The best film**

Which film from 4a) do you like: A, B or C? (Circle,) then tell each other.
Welchen Film aus 4a) magst du: A, B oder C? Umkreise, dann sprecht darüber.

I like film A / B / C best. I think it looks interesting / funny / exciting.

▶ Extra practice 9, p. 96

7 Viewing **Film time**

a) *Welchen Film haben die Kinder gewählt? Sieh den Trailer an. Umkreise den richtigen Namen.*

A Doctor Meow   B Dex 2000   C Agent Green 3

b) *Sieh dir den Trailer noch einmal an. Umkreise das richtige Wort.*

1 The film is about an agent /(a robot).
2 He is clever / kind.
3 Friends / heroes are important in the film too.
4 The film takes place in Brighton / London.
5 The film is scary / funny.

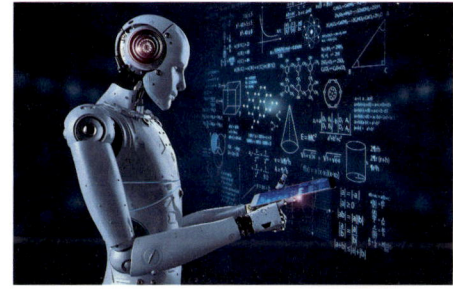

My task

8 A film trailer   ▶ Digital help

a) *Arbeitet in kleinen Gruppen. Wählt einen Film, den ihr alle mögt. Schreibt Sätze für einen Filmtrailer. Ihr könnt die Wörter in der Box nutzen.*   ▶ Wordbank 5, p. 164

This is	an action film • a cartoon • a science fiction film	about	animals • friends • superheroes.
It takes place[1] in	London • New York • a school • a skatepark.		
The main character[2] is	a dog • a robot • a singer • a superhero.		
It's the	best • coolest • funniest	film	of the year.
It's	cooler • funnier • more interesting	than	'Spiderman'.

b) *Nehmt euren Filmtrailer mit dem Handy auf und spielt ihn der Klasse vor.*

---
[1] **take place** *stattfinden*   [2] **main character** *Hauptdarsteller/in*

Gaming

1 What do you think?

Your teacher reads a sentence. Stand up if you agree. Sit down if you don't.
Deine Lehrkraft liest einen Satz vor. Stehe auf, wenn du zustimmst. Setze dich hin oder bleibe sitzen, wenn du nicht zustimmst.

1 Video games are boring.
2 Computer gaming is better than console gaming.

3 Puzzle[1] games aren't real games.
4 Adventure[2] games are the best.

2 Listening **Where do I go next?**

a) Before you listen *Sieh dir die Karte des Onlinespiels an. Nenne einen der Begriffe. Dein/e Partner/in zeigt darauf. Wechselt euch ab.*

b) *Sunita hilft Finn bei dem Onlinespiel. Höre zu und folge der gelben Linie.*

c) *Höre noch einmal zu und sieh dir das Bild an. Lies die Wegbeschreibungen 1–5 und setze den richtigen Buchstaben aus dem Bild ein.*

1 turn right   C   2 go up ☐   3 go across ☐

4 turn left ☐   5 go straight on ☐

▶ Extra practice 10–12, pp. 97–98

---

[1] **puzzle** *Rätsel*   [2] **adventure** *Abenteuer*

3 Reading Sunita's trophies

a) Read Sunita's chat with Finn. (Circle) the trophy that they talk about.
Lies Sunitas Chat mit Finn. Umkreise die Trophäe, über die sie sprechen.

b) Find Sunita's other trophies. Write the letter of the trophy. *Finde Sunitas andere Trophäen. Schreibe den Buchstaben auf.*

1 It's the one to the right of trophy e.   **f**

2 It's the one between trophies a and c.   ☐

3 It's the one under trophy b.   ☐

4 It's the one to the left of trophy b.   ☐

Finn	___	Oh wow, you have so many trophies!
Sunita	_	Thanks!
Finn	___	What's the one to the right of trophy "d" for?
Sunita	_	That's for a perfect game!
Finn	___	Cool! 😍😍😍
Sunita	_	😌

My task

4 Game designer
▶ Digital help

a) *Verfolge den gelben Weg in diesem Onlinespiel. Beschreibe, wie man ans Ziel kommt. Nutze die Wörter in der Box. Beginne so:* Start near the apple tree. Then ...

go straight on	
go up / down the	stairs • mountain
go across the	bridge • river
turn left / right at the	house • mountains • river • tree • wall

b) *Möchtest du deinen eigenen Weg einzeichnen und beschreiben? Gehe auf* S. 98.

gital quiz **Ich kann** Wege beschreiben und Wegbeschreibungen verstehen. ✅

Zane online

1 Reading **Too much of a good thing?**

a) Before you read **Answer the questions. Then tell each other about your online time.** *Beantworte die Fragen. Dann sprecht darüber wie lange ihr online seid.*

1 How much time do you spend online every day?

I spend about _____ minutes / hours online every day.

2 What do you do?

I _____ .

- chat with friends
- play games
- watch videos

▶ Wordbank 6, p. 165

b) **Look at the pictures. Who can you see? (Circle) the correct names.**
Sieh dir die Bilder an. Wen kannst du sehen? Umkreise die richtigen Namen.

I can see Lily / Noah / Sunita / Zane / Noah's mum / Zane's mum.

c) **Now read the story.** *Nun lies die Geschichte.*

"Oh, I'm so bored!" thought Zane. "What
am I going to do all day?"
Zane was at home because he
had a bad cough and his head hurt.
5 He opened a video app and watched
a video. It was really funny! He watched
the next one ... and the next one ...
Then it was lunch time.
"Your dad isn't at home," said Zane's mum.
10 "And I have to go to town. Are you
going to be OK?"
"Yes, I am, Mum," said Zane.

After lunch Zane watched videos again.
When his dad came home, Zane was
15 still on his phone.
"No more screen time today, Zane!"
said his dad.
"You know the rules – one hour a day!"

The next week Zane watched videos
20 every evening on his phone – sometimes
until very late.
"You look tired, Zane," his mum said.
"What's wrong?"
"I'm OK," Zane said. That wasn't true.

25 The next weekend his friends went swimming,
but Zane didn't want to go.
"Sorry, I can't," he said to Lily on the phone.
"I must go now. Bye!"
Lily was surprised.

30 "I'm worried," she said to Sunita.
"Zane didn't come to Noah's house last
weekend and he didn't do his history
homework. Something is wrong!"
"Finn said Zane watches lots of videos now,"
35 answered Sunita.
"Right," said Lily. "I'm going to visit Zane."

Zane was surprised and not very happy
to see Lily.
"I told you I was busy," he said.
40 "Too busy for your friends, Zane?" asked Lily.
Zane looked angry. "Please go, Lily."

2 Zane's problem

Match the sentence parts. Draw lines. *Ordne die Satzteile einander zu. Ziehe Linien.*

1 Zane's problem started when	a watched videos every evening.
2 He watched	b he didn't want to see her.
3 The next week he	c something was wrong with Zane.
4 Lily knew that	d videos all day.
5 Lily went to see Zane, but	e he was at home with a bad cough.

3 The story ending

Read the three possible story endings. (Circle) the ending that you like the best:
A, B or C? *Sieh dir die drei möglichen Enden der Geschichte an. Umkreise das Ende, das dir am besten gefällt: A, B oder C.*

A	B	C
Lily looked sad. "I'm sorry, Lily," Zane said. "I can't stop. I need help."	"No, Zane!" Lily said. "I'm worried about you. Friends are more important than videos."	"I don't want to be your friend, Zane," said Lily. "But Lily …," Zane looked surprised.

4 Words and phrases in the story

What do these words and phrases mean? Draw lines.
Was bedeuten diese Wörter und Sätze? Ziehe Linien.

> Need help?
> Read the words
> in the story.

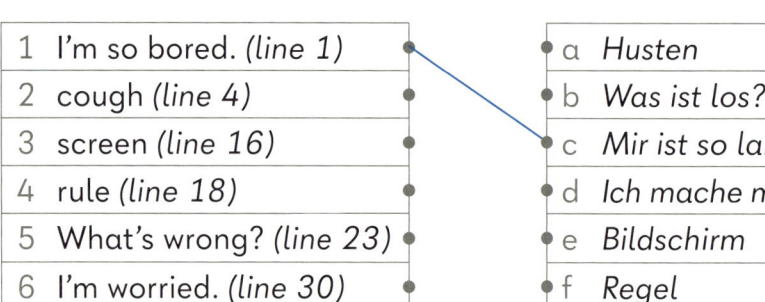

1 I'm so bored. *(line 1)*	a *Husten*
2 cough *(line 4)*	b *Was ist los?*
3 screen *(line 16)*	c *Mir ist so langweilig.*
4 rule *(line 18)*	d *Ich mache mir Sorgen.*
5 What's wrong? *(line 23)*	e *Bildschirm*
6 I'm worried. *(line 30)*	f *Regel*

5 Life skills **Plan your screen time**

a) **How do you feel when you spend a lot of time online?** (Circle.) *Wie fühlst du dich, wenn du sehr viel Zeit online verbringst? Umkreise das Wort, das für dich passt.*

I feel …   1 great.   2 tired.   3 bored.   4 OK.   5 horrible.

b) **What do you think is the best tip for Zane?** (Circle) it.
Was denkst du ist der beste Tipp für Zane? Umkreise den Tipp.

1 Go outside.   2 Meet your friends.   3 Put your phone in the living room at night.

c) **Plan your screen time for next week. Write the number. Tell each other.** *Plane deine Bildschirmzeit für nächste Woche. Schreibe die Stundenzahl auf. Redet darüber.*

I'm going to spend _____ hours on my phone next week.

Digital quiz   **Ich kann** über Bildschirmzeit sprechen.

Brighton stories: After-school fun

1 After-school activities

Before you watch **Sieh dir die Bilder an.**
Welche Aktivität möchtest du machen? Schreibe sie auf. Redet darüber.

A

B

C

D

gardening[1]

photography

sewing[2]

street dancing

I'd like to do _____.

2 Viewing **A group activity**

a) **Sieh dir den ersten Teil des Films an. Umkreise die richtige Antwort in Blau.**

1 The kids decided to do street dancing / photography.
2 Emir / Daisy wasn't very happy about the activity at first.
3 The person who learns the most and dances well wins / is boring!

b) **Sieh dir den letzten Teil des Films an. Schreibe D (Daisy), E (Emir) oder G (Gloria).**

1 Who learned the most? _____   2 Who was the winner? _____

3 Now you

What can you teach each other? Write, then talk. *Was könnt ihr einander beibringen? Schreibt es auf, dann sprecht darüber.*

badminton • basketball • boxing • swimming • taking photos

I'm good at _____. I can teach you!

That's cool!

No thanks! I don't like ...

---

[1] **gardening** *Gartenarbeit* [2] **sewing** *Nähen*

Give your opinion

1   Listening   **What do you think?**

a) **The five friends are talking about a new show. Listen and read.**
Die fünf Freunde sprechen über eine neue Show. Höre zu und lies.

Zane   I think *Scout's World* is the best show ever! It's so funny.

Lily   That isn't true. In my opinion it isn't funny at all!

Sunita   Really, Lily? I agree with Zane. It's a great show. I love it!
What do you think, Finn?

Finn   You're right, Sunita. It's a cool show. Noah, do you like it?

Noah   No, I don't. I don't agree with Zane. It's boring!

b) **Match. Draw lines.** *Ordne zu. Ziehe Linien.*

1 give an opinion	2 ask for an opinion	3 agree	4 don't agree

a I agree. You're right.	b I think … In my opinion …	c I don't agree. That isn't true.	d What do you think?

2   Speaking   **I think …**

a) **What do you think? Write a sentence. The words in the box can help you.** *Was denkst du? Schreibe einen Satz. Die Wörter in der Box können dir helfen.*

football • pizza • the colour pink • shopping	is	boring • cool • cute • easy • fun • hard • horrible • interesting • scary • …
onions • cats • dogs • school uniforms	are	

I think _____.

b) **Tell each other. Do you agree or not?** *Redet darüber. Seid ihr einer Meinung oder nicht?*

I think cats are horrible!

I agree.

I don't agree. I think cold weather is horrible.

Plan and present an activity day

Step 1 ▶ Digital help

Arbeitet zu zweit. Ihr möchtet einen Projekttag in der Schule planen. Wählt eine Aktivität aus der Box oder überlegt euch eine andere Aktivität.

Activity day ideas
- a sports competition
- a knitting day
- a party
- a concert

Step 2 ▶ Digital help

Ergänzt die Lücken zu eurem Projekttag.

Name of activity day: _____ When: _____

Where: _____ Cost[1]: _____

Step 3 ▶ Digital help

Erstellt ein Poster zu eurem Projekttag. Nutzt eure Notizen aus Step 2. Fügt Bilder hinzu.

A table tennis competition
Do you like table tennis?
Join[2] our competition!
It's going to be a great day!
Where: in the sports hall
When: Saturday, January 18th, at 10.30
Cost: It's free!

Step 4

Was plant ihr an eurem Projekttag zu tun? Ändert die Wörter in Blau. Schreibt einen eigenen Text in euer Arbeitsheft. Tragt dann eure Pläne einer anderen Gruppe oder der Klasse vor.

> *We're going to have a table tennis competition. It's going to be in the sports hall, on Saturday, January 18th. It's going to start at half past ten. It's going to be a lot of fun!*

---

[1] **cost** *Kosten*   [2] **join** *mitmachen*

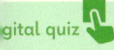 **Ich kann** einen Projekttag planen und präsentieren. ✓

1 Language **After school**

Lies das Gespräch. Ergänze die Sätze mit dem going to-Futur. Die Wörter in der Box können dir helfen.

> 'm going to (2x) • 's going to (2x) • 're going to (2x)

Finn ____ What a long day! What are you going to do after school?

Sunita ____ (1) *I'm going to* have dinner and then (2) I_____ play some computer games with Nish. After that (3) he_____ help me with the French homework. What about you?

Finn ____ It's my grandpa's birthday, so (4) we_____ talk online. (5) He_____ open his presents. Then (6) we_____ make a pizza. And after that (7) I_____ play some computer games too!

Sunita ____ Great – see you online later.

2 Reading **Comments about a new song**

a) *Lies die Kommentare. Ordne sie den Namen zu. Ziehe Linie von den Namen zur Sprechblase.*

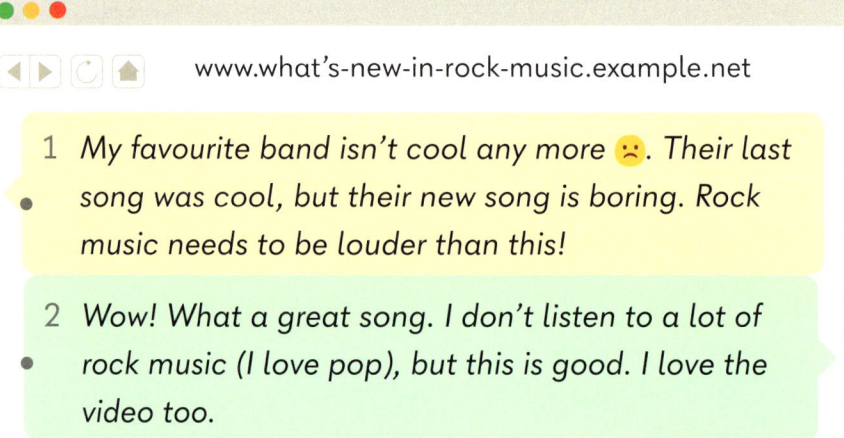

PopQueen

Rock_4eva

1 My favourite band isn't cool any more 😦. Their last song was cool, but their new song is boring. Rock music needs to be louder than this!

2 Wow! What a great song. I don't listen to a lot of rock music (I love pop), but this is good. I love the video too.

b) *Lies noch einmal Kommentar 1 in a). Umkreise die richtigen Antworten in Blau.*

1 The new song is quieter / more exciting than the band's other songs.

2 The old songs were worse / better than the new song.

Check

3 Language **Which show do you want to see?**

a) **Compare the shows. Use the words in the box.**
Vergleiche die Shows. Nutze die Wörter in der Box.

better • cooler • more interesting

1 *Billy Elliot* is _____ (cool) than *Oliver!*

2 *Oliver!* is _____ (interesting) than *Mary Poppins*.

3 *Billy Elliot* is _____ (good) *Mary Poppins*.

b) **Compare the shows. Use the words in the box.**
Vergleiche die Shows. Nutze die Wörter in der Box.

best • longest • most interesting

1 *Oliver!* is the _____ (long) show.

2 *Billy Elliot* is the _____ (good) show.

3 *Billy Elliot* is the _____ (interesting) show.

4 Words **A secret level**

Ich kann Wege beschreiben und Wegbeschreibungen verstehen.

Sunita hilft Finn bei einem Computerspiel. Ergänze ihre Sätze. Nutze die Wörter in der Box.

across • between • straight • turn

1 Go _____ the silver bridge. 2 Then _____ right.

3 Go _____ on. 4 Stop _____ the two trees.

Check

Partner page

8 My task **Make plans for the weekend**   ► page 77

Partner B: Look at your calendar. Find a time to meet Partner A. Partner A starts.
Sieh dir deinen Kalender an. Finde einen Termin, um Partner/in A zu treffen. Partner/in A beginnt.

Partner A _____ Hi! What are you going to do
on Saturday afternoon?
Can we play football?

Partner B _____ Sorry, I can't. I'm going to ...
What about Saturday morning?

Partner A _____ Sorry, I can't. I'm going to ...
What about Sunday afternoon?

Partner B _____ Good idea! Let's meet at ...

Partner A _____ Great! See you then!

Partner B _____ OK, bye!

Saturday
go shopping
with dad   3.00

Sunday
watch a film
at the cinema   10.30

Extra practice

Extra practice 1   ► page 73

Match the times. Draw lines. *Ordne die Uhrzeiten einander zu. Verbinde.*

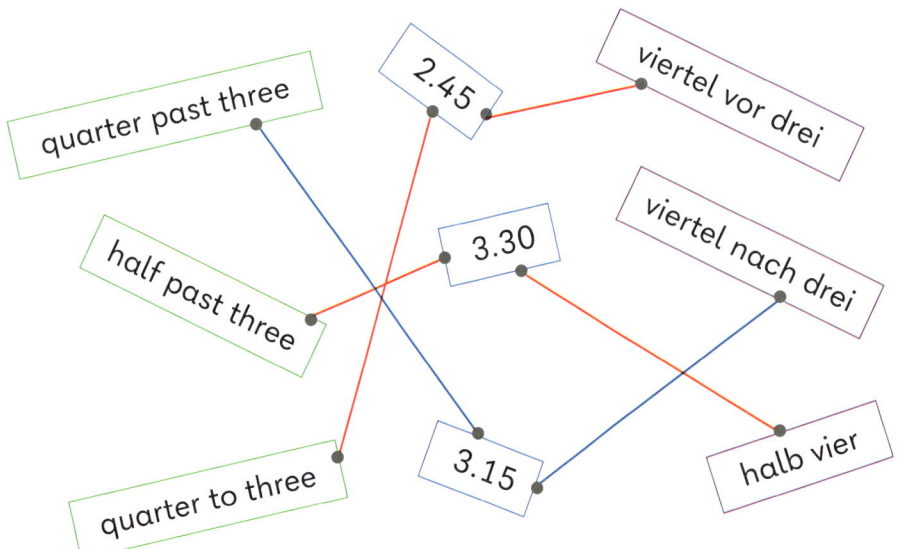

quarter past six:
viertel nach sechs

half past six:
*halb **sieben***

quarter to six:
*viertel **vor** sechs*

quarter past three   2.45   viertel vor drei

half past three   3.30   viertel nach drei

quarter to three   3.15   halb vier

▶ page 73

Extra practice 2

Match the times. Draw lines. *Ordne die Zeiten einander zu. Verbinde.*

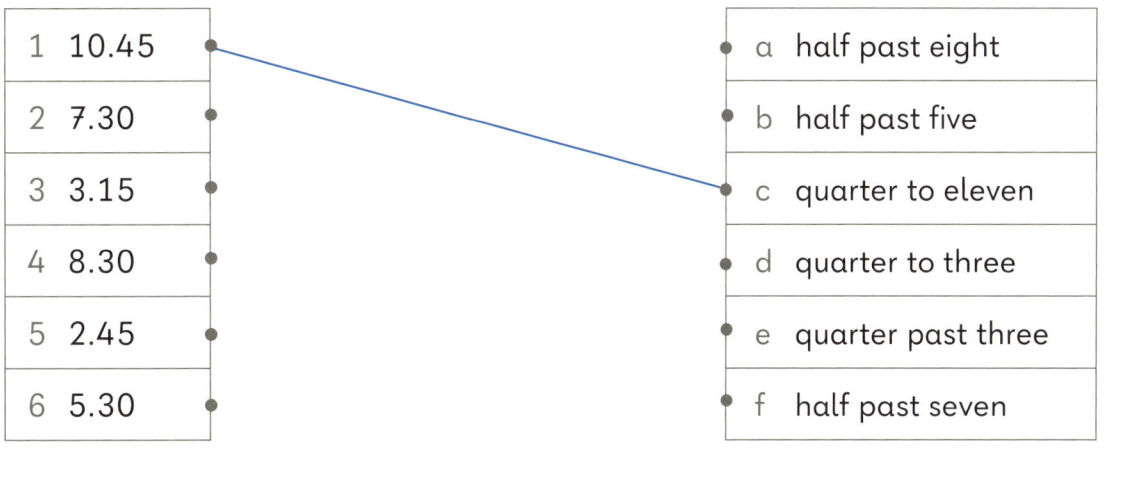

1 10.45	a half past eight
2 7.30	b half past five
3 3.15	c quarter to eleven
4 8.30	d quarter to three
5 2.45	e quarter past three
6 5.30	f half past seven

▶ page 73

Extra practice 3

Listen to six conversations. Number the times from 1–6.

Höre den sechs Gesprächen zu. Ordne die Uhrzeiten von 1–6.

3.20	12.25	5.40
a _____	b _____	c __1__
8:50	11.05	1.35
d _____	e _____	f _____

Extra practice 4 ▶ page 76

What are the students going to do at the weekend? (Circle) the right
going to-form. *Was planen die Kinder am Wochenende zu tun? Umkreise die richtige going to-Form.*

1   Sunita and Nish is going to / are going to play video games.

2   Noah is going to / are going to listen to music.

3   Amir is going to / are going to go shopping.

4   Edek and Kyle is going to / are going to eat pizza.

5   Poppy is going to / are going to do her homework.

6   Livia and her sister is going to / are going to watch a film.

Extra practice 5 ▶ page 77

Speed dating *Frage andere in deiner Klasse, was ihre Pläne für den nächsten Freitag sind. Finde Kinder für drei Aktivitäten. Schreibe ihre Namen auf.*

Are you going to do a sport?

No, I'm not.

Are you going to watch a show?

Yes, I am.

Activity	Name
Are you going to do a sport?	
Are you going to watch a show?	
Are you going to cook?	
Are you going to do homework?	
Are you going to meet friends?	

▶ page 77

Extra practice 6

a) Before you listen *Sieh dir das Bild an. Was siehst du? Umkreise die richtigen Wörter.*

1 I can see Finn / Noah and his dad / mum .

2 Finn is on the phone / computer.

b) *Höre Finn und Zane zu. Lies die Fragen von Finns Mutter und Finns Antworten. Sind Finns Antworten richtig? Mache ein Häkchen (✓) bei den richtigen Antworten und ein Kreuz (✗) bei den falschen Antworten.*

Finn's mum	Finn	✓ / ✗
1 Was ist schade? Hat Zane schon etwas vor?	*Ja, er hat heute schon etwas vor.*	✓
2 Ist Zane auch morgen beschäftigt?	*Ja, er ist morgen auch beschäftigt.*	
3 Was ist mit seiner Oma?	*Sie sagt, ich kann nicht kommen.*	
4 Habt ihr etwas ausgemacht?	*Nein, er ist zu beschäftigt.*	

Extra practice 7

▶ page 79

Compare the people in the band. *Vergleiche die Menschen in der Band.*

1 Ellis has __*longer*__ (long) hair than Alex.

2 Ellis is _____ (tall) than Sam.

3 Alex is _____ (short) than Charlie.

4 Sam's guitar is _____ (small) than Charlie's guitar.

5 Alex is _____ (strong) than Sam.

▶ page 79

Extra practice 8

Complete the sentences with the correct form of the words in the brackets.
Vervollständige die Sätze mit der richtigen Form der Wörter in Klammern.

1

Fish are _quieter_ (quiet) than monkeys.

2

Horses are _____ (fast) than elephants.

3

Seagulls are _____ (loud) than cats.

4

Hamsters are _____ (slow) than dogs.

5

Lions are _____ (strong) than snakes.

6

Parrots are _____ (small) than rabbits.

▶ page 80

Extra practice 9

a) *Lies den Beispielsatz. Sage dann, was du denkst. Setze* electro, classical *und* rock *in eine für dich passende Reihenfolge.*

I think electro is cooler than classical, but rock is the coolest.

I think _____ is cooler than _____, but _____

is the coolest.

b) *Setze* action films, cartoons *und* science fiction films *in eine für dich passende Reihenfolge.*

I think _____ are more interesting than _____,

but _____ are the most interesting.

▶ page 82

Extra practice 10

Write the right words under the pictures.
Schreibe die richtigen Wörter unter die Bilder.

bridge • dragon • house • mountain • river • stairs • tree • wall

1

_____

2

_____

3

_____

4

_____

5

_____

6

_____

7

_____

8

_____

▶ page 82

Extra practice 11

Help Scout get to the sandwich. Complete the directions. *Hilf Scout zum Sandwich zu gelangen. Ergänze die Wegbeschreibung.*

left • next to • past • right • straight on

Scout, you need to go (1) _____

and then turn (2) _____ at the bin[1].

Then turn left and go (3) _____ the

family with the dog, turn (4) _____

at the castle and it's (5) _____

the bin.

[1] **bin** *Mülltonne*

▶ page 82

Extra practice 12

Complete the directions. Use the words in the box. *Vervollständige die Richtungshinweise. Nutze die Wörter in der Box.*

across • down • into • up

1 _____ the shop

2 _____ the stairs

3 _____ the stairs

4 _____ the street

4 My task **Game designer**

▶ Page 83

b) *Hier kannst du deinen eigenen Weg einzeichnen und beschreiben.*

Unit 3

Activities and games

▶ p. 72	**panto** (*kurz für* **pantomime**)	*(in Großbritannien)* ein lustiges, traditionelles, meist zu Weihnachten aufgeführtes Theaterstück, bes. für Kinder
	zip wire (*kurz auch: zip*)	die Seilrutsche

a girl on a zip wire

▶ p. 73	**insect**	das Insekt
	lots (of)	viel/e
	half past two	halb drei
	quarter past two	viertel nach zwei
	quarter to two	viertel vor zwei
	seat	der (Sitz-)Platz

quarter to 7

quarter past 7

half past 7

Topic 1

dragon	der Drache

dragons

(to) knit	stricken
(to) create	(er)schaffen, erstellen
toy	das Spielzeug
(to) practise	üben
goat	die Ziege

a goat

photography	die Fotografie *(Hobby)*, das Fotografieren
castle	die Burg

(to) act	aufführen, spielen

▶ p. 75	**I'm going to choose ...**	Ich werde ... (aus)wählen. / Ich habe vor, ... zu wählen / auszuwählen.
	(to) choose	(aus)wählen

▶ p. 76 | **Do you have any plans?** | Habt ihr / Hast du (irgendwelche) Pläne?
| **not (…) anything** | nichts
| **evening** | der Abend
| **tomorrow** | morgen
▶ p. 77 | **date** | die Verabredung, das Date *(auch die Person, mit der man ausgeht)*

Topic 2

▶ p. 78 | **classical (music)** | die klassische Musik
| **acoustic** | akustisch
| **pop (music)** | der Pop, die Popmusik
| **(to) agree (with sb./sth.)** | jm. zustimmen; mit etwas einverstanden sein
▶ p. 79 | **slower/faster than …** | langsamer/schneller als …
| **better** | besser
| **worse** | schlechter, schlimmer
▶ p. 80 | **cartoon** | der Zeichentrickfilm; der/das Comic; der Cartoon
| **the most exciting …** | der/die/das aufregendste …
| **exciting** | aufregend
| **worst** | der/die/das schlechteste, schlimmste; am schlechtesten, am schlimmsten

Topic 3

▶ p. 82 | **puzzle** | das Rätsel
| **real** | echt, wirklich
| **bridge** | die Brücke

a **bridge across** a river

| **stairs** *(pl)* | die Treppe; die (Treppen-)Stufen
| **river** | der Fluss
| **mountain** | der Berg
| **(to) turn right/left** | (nach) rechts/links abbiegen

Turn left. Turn right. Go straight on.

| **across** a bridge | über eine Brücke
| **up** | hinauf, hoch
| **straight on** | geradeaus (weiter)
▶ p. 83 | **trophy** | die Trophäe; der Pokal

trophies

| **the one** | der/die/das(-jenige)
| **between** | zwischen

Story

► p. 84	(to) spend (time), *simple past:* spent	(Zeit) verbringen
	(to) be bored	sich langweilen
	cough	der Husten
	no	kein, keine; verboten
	screen	der Bildschirm; die Leinwand *(Kino)*
	screen time	Bildschirmzeit; Zeit am Handy
	rule	die Regel
	one hour a day	eine Stunde pro Tag
► p. 85	until	bis *(zeitlich)*
	What's wrong?	Was ist los? / Was ist das Problem?
	true	wahr, richtig
	must	müssen
	(to) be worried (about)	beunruhigt sein, besorgt sein (wegen)
	do your homework	die Hausaufgaben machen
► p. 86	(to) read	lesen
	outside	draußen; nach draußen
	night	die Nacht

a computer screen

Study skills

► p. 88	world	die Welt
	the best show ever	die beste Show überhaupt / die beste Show, die man sich wünschen kann
	opinion	die Meinung
	in my opinion	meiner Meinung nach

Unit 4
Celebrate!

Food is an important part of this festival.

This festival has a lot of colour.

1 Listening **Celebrations in Britain**

a) Before you listen *Sieh dir die Fotos an. Lies die Sätze. Nenne dein Lieblingsfoto.*

> *I like photo B the best.*

> *My favourite photo is C.*

b) *Höre zu. Ordne die Namen der Feste den Fotos zu. Schreibe A–D in die Tabelle.*

1 Holi (Festival of Colours)   **B**   3 Notting Hill Carnival[2]   ☐

2 Eid al-Fitr (Festival of breaking the fast[1])   ☐   4 Guy Fawkes Night (Bonfire Night)   ☐

▶ Extra practice 1, p. 124

¹ **breaking the fast** *Fastenbrechen*   ² **carnival** *Karneval*

Nach dieser Unit kann ich ...

○ über Feste in Großbritannien und
   anderen Ländern sprechen
○ ein Festessen beschreiben
○ über Festvorbereitungen und
   Familienfeiern reden
○ Präsentationen planen und üben

Unit task ✓

○ ein Fest präsentieren

Fireworks are important for this festival.

People play music and dance at this fun parade.

2 Speaking **Your celebrations**

a) **Write about a celebration that you like.** *Schreibe über ein Fest, das dir gefällt.*

My celebration is _____.

Halloween • Hanukkah • Christmas • ...

There is _____.

a parade • nice food • chocolate • music • ...

There are _____.

fireworks • decorations • presents • ...

b) **Tell each other about your celebrations.** *Erzählt einander über eure Feste.*

Special meals

1 Reading **Ramadan and Eid al-Fitr**

a) Before you read **What do you know about Ramadan and Eid al-Fitr? Circle two correct answers.** *Was weißt du über Ramadan und Eid al-Fitr? Umkreise zwei richtige Antworten.*

1 Some people fast for Ramadan.
2 For Ramadan some people eat in the morning and at night.

3 Eid al-Fitr is a festival of colours.
4 At Eid al-Fitr people go to a parade.

b) **Read the conversation. Then circle the right answers in 1–4.**
Lies das Gespräch. Umkreise dann die richtigen Antworten in 1–4.

1 Noah eats / doesn't eat lunch with Zane.
2 Zane and his sister do / don't fast.
3 Fasting is important to Zane's dad / mum.
4 Zane likes / doesn't like celebrating Eid al-Fitr.

Noah	Hi, Zane! Can I eat lunch with you?
Zane	Sure!
Noah	What are you doing tonight?
Zane	We're going to have a special dinner tonight. You know, for the month of Ramadan.
Noah	I see you aren't fasting.
Zane	No, dad fasts, but mum and Holly and I don't fast.
Noah	Can I ask you – is it hard for your dad when he's working in the cafe?
Zane	Ha, that's what everyone asks! But it's important to him. And he eats in the morning and at night.
Noah	Do you all celebrate Eid al-Fitr?
Zane	Yes, we all go to the celebration meal. It's great!

c) **Match the words (1–4) to the correct definitions (A–D). Draw lines.**
Ordne die Wörter (1–4) den richtigen Bedeutungen (A–D) zu. Ziehe Linien.

1 dinner		A	when you have fun on a special day
2 (to) fast		B	the meal in the evening
3 (to) celebrate		C	the meal in the afternoon
4 lunch		D	when you don't eat food for some time

2 Words **Food**

a) Revision (Circle) five food words. *Umkreise fünf Wörter, die Essen beschreiben.*

> bread • British • car • cake • melon • message • ring • rice • salad • sand

b) **Write the words in the box under the pictures.**
Schreibe die Wörter in der Box unter die richtigen Bilder.

> curry • juice • lamb • pork

A   B

l _ _ _   j _ _ _ _

C   D

c _ _ _ _   p _ _ _

c) **Close your books. How many things in b) can you remember? Can you write them?** *Schließt eure Bücher. Wie viele Wörter aus b) konntet ihr euch merken? Könnt ihr sie schreiben?*

▶ Extra practice 2, p. 125   ▶ Extra practice 3, p. 126

3 Mediation **An invitation to Eid al-Fitr**

Read Zane's invitation. Then complete Finn's message to his dad.
Lies Zanes Einladung. Ergänze dann Finns Nachricht an seinen Vater.

Hello friends

I'd like to invite you to Eid al-Fitr. We're going to celebrate with my family and neighbours.

Day: Sunday 1st May
Time: 1 o'clock
Place: The garden behind the mosque

We're going to eat an amazing meal together!
Zane

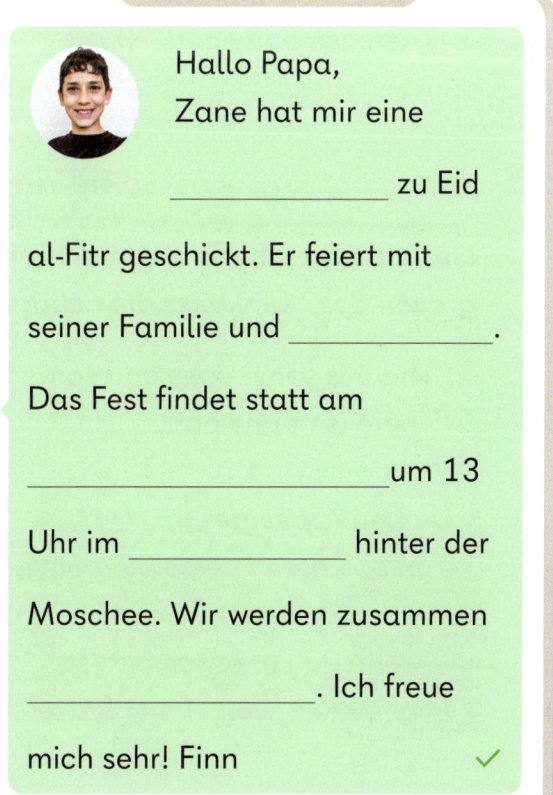

Hallo Papa,
Zane hat mir eine _____ zu Eid al-Fitr geschickt. Er feiert mit seiner Familie und _____. Das Fest findet statt am _____ um 13 Uhr im _____ hinter der Moschee. Wir werden zusammen _____. Ich freue mich sehr! Finn

4 Listening **Before the celebration**

a) Before you listen **Have you ever celebrated Eid al-Fitr? Write, then tell each other.**
Hast du schon mal Eid al-Fitr gefeiert? Schreibe es auf. Erzählt es dann einander.

Yes, I have.	I celebrated it … in 20… / last year / with my family / with friends / …
No, I haven't.	I think it's interesting. / I'd like to celebrate it / …

b) **Listen. Zane and the other kids talk about three topics.
(Circle).** *Höre zu. Zane und die anderen Kinder sprechen
über drei Themen. Umkreise sie.*

> clothes • decorations • food • money • tickets • weather

c) **Listen again. Who says sentences 1–4? (Circle) the
correct name.** *Höre noch einmal zu. Wer sagt die
Sätze 1–4? Umkreise den richtigen Namen.*

> Finn • Lily • Noah • Sunita • Zane

1 Don't bring any food!   3 There are some salads.
2 There isn't any pork.   4 There is some cake and some bread.

5 Looking at language *some* and *any*

Erklär-
film

Lies die Sätze 1 und 2. Unterstreiche some *und* any. *Wie lautet die Regel in der
grauen Box? Umkreise die richtigen Wörter in Blau.*

1 There is some cake and some bread.
2 There isn't any pork.

Du benutzt **some**
– in *bejahten / verneinten* Sätzen,
– wenn du jemandem etwas anbietest,
– wenn du um etwas bittest.
In *bejahten / verneinten* Sätzen verwendest du **any**.

*Would you like
some chips?*

*Yes, please. Can I
have some fish too?*

▶ **Extra practice 4–5, p. 126**

6 Ready for Eid al-Fitr

Zane and his family are getting ready for the Eid meal. (Circle) the correct words.
Zane und seine Familie bereiten sich auf das Essen zu Eid vor. Umkreise die richtigen Wörter.

Zane, would you like (some)/ any lemonade?

No thanks, Mum. I still have some / any juice.

Mum, can I have some / any chocolate?

No, you can't have some / any chocolate now, Holly.

7 Speaking **What would you like?**

a) Read the conversation and listen. *Lies das Gespräch und höre zu.*

Zane ____ Would you like some potato curry?
Finn ____ Yes, please. I'd like some rice and some yoghurt, too.
Zane ____ OK, here you are. Would you like a lamb kebab?
Finn ____ No, thanks. Can I have a little salad please?
Zane ____ Of course. What about some fruit?
Finn ____ Yes, please. May I have some melon?
Zane ____ Yes, here you are. Enjoy your meal!

b) Practice the conversation. *Übt das Gespräch zu zweit.*

My task

8 An invitation to a special meal

a) Schreibe eine Einladung zu einem besonderen Essen auf Englisch. Ändere die blauen Wörter in der Einladung rechts. ▸ Wordbank 7, p. 166.

b) Gallery walk *Lies alle Einladungen. Welches Essen hört sich am besten an? Erzähle es der Klasse.*

I like Torge's meal best.

▸ **Digital help** ⬇

Hello Charlie
I'd like to invite you to a special meal at my home on Sunday at 6 o'clock. We're going to have 'Maultaschen'. It's like ravioli. We eat it with salad. Then we're going to eat apple cake with cream. It's my aunt's recipe. Can you come?
Sasha

Meera ♥ Ben

1 Listening **A big celebration**

a) **Before you listen** *Sunita und Lily sprechen über eine Feier für Meera und Ben. Über welche Feier sprechen sie? Umkreise.*

> a birthday • Diwali • Halloween • a wedding[1]

b) *Höre zu. Überprüfe deine Antwort bei b).*

c) *Höre noch einmal zu. Wähle die richtige Antwort.*

1 Sunita has / doesn't have new clothes for the celebration.
2 Lily, Zane and Noah can / can't come to the celebration.
3 Sunita wants an idea for decorations / a surprise[2] for her mum and Ben.
4 Lily talks about the presentation[3] / song on Zane's birthday.

2 Reading **Sunita's surprise**

a) **Before you read** *Was ist Sunitas Überraschung für Ben und Meera?*

It's a _____ .

> book • presentation • small pet • trip

b) *Lies Sunitas Liste. Schreibe, warum sie froh ist und warum nicht. Nutze has / hasn't.*

Sunita is happy because ...

1 she *has*_____ asked Willow for help.

2 she _____ thought of some nice stories.

3 she _____ found photos of her mum and Ben.

1 ask Willow for help
2 think of some nice stories
3 find photos of Mum and Ben

4 find some good music
5 practise the presentation
6 ask my friends what they think

Sunita isn't happy because ...

4 she *hasn't*_____ found any good music.

5 she _____ practised the presentation.

6 she _____ asked her friends what they think.

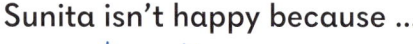

[1] **wedding** *Hochzeit*   [2] **surprise** *Überraschung*   [3] **presentation** *Vorführung, Präsentation*

Erklär-film

3 Walk around **Why are you happy?**

How do you feel? Complete the sentence. Use the ideas in the boxes. Tell each other. *Wie fühlst du dich?* Happy *oder* unhappy? *Ergänze den Satz. Nutze die Ideen in den Boxen. Erzählt es einander.*

😌 I've talked to my best friend.
😌 I've just had my favourite lesson.

😦 I haven't finished my homework.
😦 I haven't had a good day.

I'm _____ because _____ .

4 Looking at language **The present perfect**

a) **Look at the sentences in 3. (Circle) the correct rule (A or B).** *Sieh dir die Sätze in 3 an. Umkreise die richtige Regel (A oder B).*

Wir verwenden das *present perfect* für etwas, dass ...
A bereits geschehen ist.   B in der Zukunft geschehen wird.

Why are you sad?

I've lost my favourite hat. It has blown away.

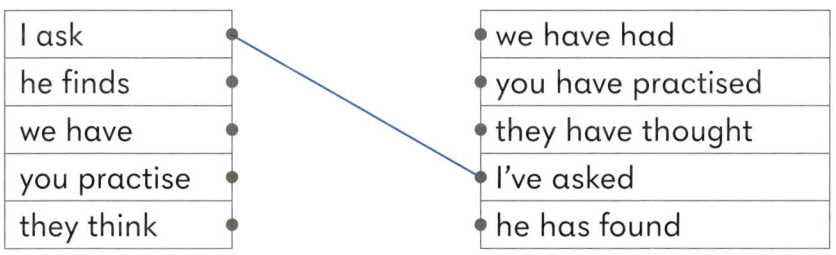

b) **Match the words on the left with the present perfect on the right. Draw lines.**
Verbinde die Wörter links mit dem present perfect *rechts.*

I ask
he finds
we have
you practise
they think

we have had
you have practised
they have thought
I've asked
he has found

▶ **Extra practice 6–9, pp. 127–128**   ▶ **Irregular verbs, pp. 170–171**

5 How do they feel?

Choose the correct words in the present perfect. (Circle) them.
Wähle die richtigen Wörter im present perfect.

1 Lily feels good. She has helped / has learned Sunita with her presentation.
2 Sunita is tired. She has talked / has worked a lot on her presentation.
3 Ben feels happy. He has worked / has learned a new song for Meera.
4 George is sad. Nobody[1] has talked / has helped to him – everybody is busy!

---

[1] **nobody** *niemand*

6   Poor George!

Ergänze die Sätze mit den Wörtern in der Box.

> bought • given • seen • slept

George   I'm tired. I haven't _____ (1 sleep¹) much. Everybody is busy.

Scout   Oh! But look! I've _____ (2 buy) a new hat to wear to it.

George   Very nice! Is that fruit? I'm hungry! They haven't

_____ (3 give) me food.

Scout   I've _____ (4 see) some fruit in your garden. I can get some.

George   Thanks Scout! You're a good friend.

7   Getting ready

a) *Partner/in B: Gehe zur Seite 124.*
Partner/in A: Lies laut vor, was Sunita zu Nish sagt.
Partner/in B liest dir danach vor, was Nish zu Sunita sagt.

> I haven't found any clothes for the wedding.
> And I haven't finished my presentation.
> But I have invited my friends!

b) *Nish und Sunita haben beide schon eine Sache getan. Welche?*

They have _____ their _____.

8   Reading   Sunita's family

Willow telefoniert mit Sunita. Wer ist bei Sunita?
Lies das Gespräch und umkreise die richtige Antwort.

A Sunita's friends   B Sunita's family   C Ben

Willow   Hi, Sunita. Have your grandparents arrived from India?
Sunita   Yes, they have. They've just got here.
Willow   Has your family from Birmingham come too?
Sunita   Yes, my aunt and uncle and cousins are here. Our house is full of people!

---

¹ sleep, slept, slept *schlafen*

Erklär-
film

9 Looking at language **The present perfect: yes/no-questions**

Match Sunita's questions to Willow's answers. Draw lines.

Ordne Sunitas Fragen Willows Antworten zu. Ziehe Linien.

1 Has Ben invited a lot of friends?	a Yes, I have.
2 Have you helped Ben with the wedding?	b Yes, he has.

10 Speaking **Today**

Ask each other these questions. Answer with: *Yes, I have or No, I haven't.*

Stellt einander diese Fragen. Antwortet mit Yes, I have *oder* No I haven't.

1 Have you had breakfast?   3 Have you smiled[1] at a teacher?

2 Have you made your bed?   4 Have you listened to music?

My task

11 Quiz **Have you ever ...?**   ▶ **Digital help**

Stellt einander die Fragen aus der Tabelle. Antwortet mit Yes, I have *oder* No, I haven't. *Schreibt den Namen der Person auf, die „Yes" sagt.*

Have you ever	been to Turkey?	_____
	eaten chips with cheese?	_____
	seen a lion?	_____
	talked to a pop star?	_____
	told a lie[2]?	_____

---

[1] smile *lächeln*   [2] a lie *Lüge*

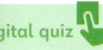
Ich kann sagen, was ich getan / nicht getan habe. ✓

Family celebrations

1 Listening **Ben and Willow's song**

Sunita's family has come together for sangeet, the day before the wedding.

Ben is so nice, but I still don't like his music!

a) Before you listen **Who is in the picture? What are they doing? Complete the sentences. Then tell each other.** *Wer ist im Bild? Was machen die Leute? Ergänze die Sätze. Erzählt es dann einander.*

I can see _____ .
_____ .

lots of people • Sunita • Meera • Ben • ...

They are _____ .
_____ .

singing • playing music • listening • ...

b) **Listen to the song.** (Circle) **the right answers.**
Höre dem Lied zu. Umkreise die richtigen Antworten.

1 Ben and Willow are singing about cheese / a clean-up day / a wedding day.
2 It's a sad / happy / angry song.

c) **What do you think about the song?** *Was denkst du über das Lied?*

I think it's boring / cool / fun / ...
I like the music / rap / words / ...
I don't like the music / rap / words ...

2 At the sangeet celebration

Read Sunita's message and match the words below. Draw lines.
Lies Sunitas Nachricht und ordne die Wörter unten einander zu. Ziehe Linien.

> After Ben's song, *someone* from his family told a story. I didn't want to sing *anything*, but I made my robot Robbie to do a special dance! After that *everyone* ate Ben's amazing meal. Then George flew onto the table – there was food *everywhere*!

someone	not ... anything	everyone	everywhere

alle	jemand	nichts	überall

▶ Extra practice 10, p. 128

My task

3 Our favourite family parties

▶ Digital help

a) (Circle) the words for family celebrations. *Umkreise die Wörter für Familienfeiern.*

> an accident • a birthday • a Christmas dinner • a kiosk • Ramadan

b) *Lies die Nachrichten. Welche Party gefällt dir? Umkreise A oder B.*

c) *Wähle eine eigene Familienfeier. Beantworte die Fragen dazu:*

What did you celebrate?

We celebrated _____.

Where was the party?

It was at _____.

What did you do?

Everyone _____.

How was it?

It was _____.

A
I loved my birthday party last year. It was at the park. Everyone ate Zane's chocolate cake and I did magic tricks. Remember we wore funny costumes? 🤣 I had a great time!

B
My family had a great party when my dad opened his cafe. It was in a hall and we had amazing music. Everyone danced! It was really fun. 😎

 Ich kann über Familienfeiern sprechen. ✓

The big day

1 Reading **What's going to happen?**

a) Before you read **Read the sentences. What do you think? Write 'yes' or 'no'.**
Lies die Sätze. Was denkst du wird passieren? Schreibe „yes" oder „no".

1 I think Meera is going to be happy.	_____
2 I think Ben is going to be late.	_____
3 I think Ben is going to wear the wrong clothes.	_____
4 I think Meera is going to wear a white dress.	_____

b) **Read the story and check if you were right in a).**
Lies die Geschichte und überprüfe, ob du in a) Recht hattest.

It's nine o'clock on Saturday morning and everyone is happy because it's Ben and Meera's big day!

Sunita is helping her mum put on her red sari.

"Mum," says Sunita, looking worried. "Have you talked to Ben today? You know he's
5 often late."

Meera smiles. "Yes, I have. Don't worry, Sunita. It's all going to be OK."
"Yes, Mum," says Sunita.

Willow is helping her dad put on his tie.
"Do I look OK?" he asks. "I haven't worn a suit and a tie for a long time!"

Your look amazing!

10 "OK," says Ben. "I just need my shoes."

"Great, Dad," says Willow. "I have a surprise. Look out of the window."

Ben looks down at the street. "It's our bikes! They look great, Willow, thank you!"

15 But then two men walk over to their bikes. "What are they doing with our bikes?" asks Willow.

"Hey! Stop!" Ben says. They run down the stairs, but the men have left – with the bikes!
20 Then they hear the door close behind them.

"The door!" says Ben. "We can't go back in. And we don't have our phones."

Willow looks down at Ben's feet. "And that's not all, Dad. You're still wearing your
25 slippers!"

"But we need to go now," says Ben. "Let's walk." They start to walk. Ben says sadly, "Meera isn't going to be happy …"

"It's OK, Dad. We're here!" says Willow.
30 "Look at Meera!"

Ben feels happy again when he sees Meera. She thinks he looks great. She laughs when she sees his slippers!

"Sorry," says Ben. "I can tell you all about it
35 later …"

"Don't worry," laughs Meera. "I'm still going to marry you – in your slippers!"

2 What happened?

Complete the sentences. Draw lines. *Ergänze die Sätze. Ziehe Linien.*

1	Ben and Meera
2	Two men took
3	Ben and Willow left their phones
4	Ben wore
5	When Meera saw Ben,

a	his slippers.
b	in the flat.
c	she laughed.
d	looked amazing.
e	their bikes.

3 Words in the text

Find the words in the story. Then match the words.
Finde die Wörter in der Geschichte. Ordne dann die Wörter einander zu. Ziehe Linien.

1	a surprise *(line 11)*
2	Don't worry. *(lines 6, 36)*
3	marry *(line 37)*

a	*heiraten*
b	*Überraschung*
c	*Mache dir keine Sorgen.*

▶ Extra practice 11, p. 128

4 A multicultural wedding

Beschreibt einander eine Person in dem Bild. Ändert die Wörter in Blau.

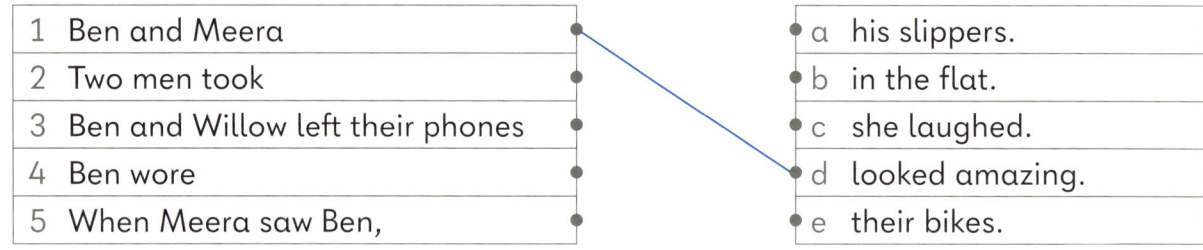

short grey hair   a blue dress   long black hair

left

right

white trousers   a blue and grey suit

> He's on the left[1].
> He's wearing white trousers.
> He has black hair.

> She's on the right[2].
> She has long brown hair.

5 Life skills Be a global citizen

Meera and Ben feiern eine multikulturelle Hochzeit. Welche unterschiedlichen Kulturen sind in deinem Leben?

I *like Sushi / ...*

Ideas
- have a friend from Ukraine
- listen to music from the USA
- watch Bollywood films
- ...

[1] **on the left** *auf der linken Seite*   [2] **on the right** *auf der rechten Seite*

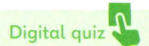 Digital quiz   **Ich kann** über verschiedene Kulturen in meinem Leben sprechen.

Brighton stories: Family and heritage[1]

1 Two truths[2] and a lie[3]

Before you watch *Lies die Sätze. Von den zwei Sätzen zu jeder Person ist einer eine Lüge. Rate. Mache ein Kreuz (✕) bei der Lüge.*

1 **Gloria**

A Her dad is from Jamaica. ☐

B Her parents met in a skating club. ☐

2 **Emir**

A His mum has a tattoo. ☐

B His dad is Kurdish[4]. ☐

3 **Daisy**

A Her great-great-grandma's name was Daisy. ☐

B All her family have always lived in Brighton. ☐

2 Viewing **Daisy's tour**

a) **Watch part 1 of the video. Check your answers from 1.** *Sieh dir Teil 1 des Videos an. Überprüfe deine Antworten von 1.*

b) **Watch part 2.** (Circle) **the right answers.** *Sieh dir Teil 2 an. Umkreise die richtigrichtigen Antworten.*

1 Do Emir, Joe and Gloria like Daisy's tour? Yes. / No.

2 What does Daisy think? At the end, Daisy thinks her family history is boring / cool.

3 Now you

a) *Spiele das Spiel „Wahrheit oder Lüge". Schreibe zwei Sätze über deine Familie. Ein Satz ist wahr, ein Satz ist gelogen. Du kannst auch eigene Sätze in dein Heft schreiben.*

My sister's hobby is _____ (bowling / singing / trampolining / ...)

Last summer we went to _____ (Berlin / Prague / my aunt's house / ...)

b) *Lest einander eure Sätze vor. Erratet ihr die Lüge?*

---

[1] **heritage** *Familiengeschichte*   [2] **truth** *Wahrheit*   [3] **lie** *Lüge*   [4] **Kurdish** *kurdisch*

Prepare and practise a presentation

1   Make your slides

Sieh dir Finns Folien für seine Präsentation an. Lies Scouts Tipp. Welche Folie ist besser: 1 oder 2? Mache ein Häkchen (✓) auf der richtigen Folie:

Deine Folien sollten haben:
- eine große Überschrift
- große Bilder
- kurze Notizen

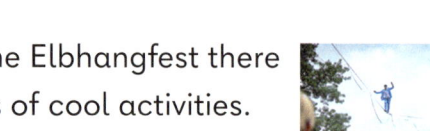

1 **The Elbhangfest**
- a big festival
- every summer
- in Dresden

2   At the Elbhangfest there are lots of cool activities. You can go to shows and music concerts. You can eat lots of great food too.

2   Make cards with short notes

Mache eine neue Folie 2 für Finn. Schreibe kurze Notizen.

The Elbhangfest: Things to do

- lots of _____

- _____

- _____

3   Practise, practise, practise!

a) *Lies die Tipps rechts. Zwei Tipps sind schlechte Tipps. Kreuzt sie an (✗).*

b) *Präsentiert Finns Folien. Übt zu zweit. Beginne so:*

Good or bad tips?
1   Don't smile. ☐
2   Speak[1] loudly. ☐
3   Don't look at your group. ☐
4   Practise in front of a mirror[2] at home. ☐
5   Watch a video of your presentation. ☐

> I'm going to talk about the Elbhangfest today. It's a …

▶ Wordbank 8, p. 167

[1] **speak** *sprechen*   [2] **mirror** *Spiegel*

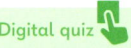 Digital quiz   **Ich kann** eine Präsentation vorbereiten und üben. ✓

Present a celebration

Step 1

Wähle eine Feier, die in deiner Familie, deiner Gegend oder in deinem Land gefeiert wird. Die Ideen in der Box helfen dir.

> a birthday • Christmas •
> Eid al-Fitr • Halloween • Hanukkah •
> Oktoberfest • a school party • ...

Step 2

▶ Digital help

Sieh dir die Fragen zu deiner Feier an und mache dir Notizen.

1 *The name of my celebration is ...*
2 *We celebrate it in ...*
3 *We celebrate it at ....*
4 ...

> 1 What's the name of your celebration?
> 2 When do you celebrate it?
> 3 Where do you celebrate it?
> 4 Do you wear special clothes?
> 5 Do you eat special food?
> 6 Is there music?

Step 3

▶ Digital help

> **Have you ...**
> ○ put pictures on your slides?
> ○ used short notes on your slides?
> ○ put big titles on your slides?

a) *Erstelle deine Folien. Überprüfe mit der Checkliste rechts, ob du auf alles geachtet hast. Mache ein Häkchen (✓).*

b) *Sieh dir die Sätze unten an. Du kannst sie für deinen Vortrag nutzen. Sind sie für den Start (S), den mittleren Teil (M) oder das Ende (E) geeignet? Schreibe S, M oder E.*

Do you have any questions?	☐	I'm going to talk about ...	☐	In this photo you can see ...	☐
Hello everyone!	S	This picture shows ...	☐	Thank you for listening.	☐

Step 4

Übt die Präsentation zu zweit. Zeigt eure Folien. Nutze Sätze aus Step 3b). Gebt einander Feedback.

▶ Wordbank 8, p. 167

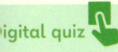 igital quiz **Ich kann ein Fest präsentieren.**

1   Listening   **A winter celebration**

Ich kann **über Feste sprechen.**

a)   Before you listen   **Look at Zane's photo. What is he celebrating?** (Circle.) *Sieh dir Zane's Foto an. Was feiert er? Umkreise.*

> Notting Hill Carnival •
> Bonfire night •
> a wedding

b)   **Now listen. What do Finn and Zane talk about?** (Circle) **two topics.**
Höre zu. Über was sprechen Finn und Zane? Umkreise zwei Themen.

> fireworks • games • music • shopping • weather

c)   **Listen again. Choose the correct answers.**
Höre noch einmal zu. Wähle die richtigen Antworten.

1   Zane's photo is from   A November   B December.
2   Zane   A always   B never   celebrates at the same park.
3   Zane often celebrates with   A his friends   B his family.
4   The weather is sometimes   A hot   B cold.

2   Language   **On the phone**

Ich kann **ein besonderes Essen beschreiben (*some* und *any*).**

Complete the sentences with *some* or *any*. *Ergänze die Sätze mit* some *oder* any.

Caller _____ Hi, we'd like five pizzas, please: one cheese pizza, two vegetable pizzas and two sausage and tomato pizzas. Please can we also get *some* _____ (1) chips?

Restaurant ___ Sure! Would you like _____ (2) sauces?

Caller _____ We don't want _____ (3) sauces, thank you.

Restaurant ___ And would you like _____ (4) drinks?

Caller _____ We don't want _____ (5) drinks, thank you.

Restaurant ___ Great. You can get your food in 30 minutes.

Check

3 Language **Before the meal**

Es ist der Nachmittag vor Eid. Was haben Zane und seine Familie schon getan, was nicht? Ergänze die Sätze mit den Wörtern in der Box.

bought • found • made • made

1 Holly hasn't _____ (find) her shoes.

2 Zane's dad has _____ (buy) some more rice.

3 Zane's parents haven't _____ (make) the curry.

4 Zane and Holly have _____ (make) the salad.

4 Reading **Welcome to Brighton!**

LILY *Hey! Check out the garden near our flat.* ✓

SUNITA *Love it!! Are you having a party?* ✓

LILY *Yes, it's a surprise party for my aunt and uncle.* ✓

ZANE *Surprise parties are the best. How are you going to surprise them?* ✓

LILY *Dad's going to meet them at the station. Then he's going to say "Let's go to the garden." In the garden we're going to jump up and say "Surprise!" I need to find some good music. We want to dance at the party!* ✓

Lies die Nachrichten zu Lilys Party. Mache ein Häkchen (✓) bei den richtigen Sätzen.

1 Zane likes surprise parties. ☐

2 Lily's dad is going to meet Lily's uncle and aunt at the station. ☐

3 The party is going to be in the flat. ☐

4 Lily is going to play some songs. ☐

Check

VARNDEAN Teen Zine

Our school magazine: by students for students

Burning the clocks

Lies den Text. Kennst du ein ähnliches Fest? Wie heißt es? _____

Burning[1] the clocks

Every year on 21st December people in
Brighton celebrate the *Burning the
Clocks* festival! There are parades
and music, and people have paper
lanterns. At the end there are
fireworks! It's a great festival.

What languages do people speak?

*Welche Sprachen hörst du in deiner
Nachbarschaft und in deiner Familie?
Schreibe die Sprachen in die Sprachwolke.*

_____ _____

_____ _____

German _____

English breakfast

*Sieh dir das Video zu englischen Frühstücksgerichten an.
Welches Frühstück würde dir am besten schmecken? Umkreise das passende Bild.*

1  2  3  4

---

[1] **burn** *(ver)brennen*

Varndean students' special meals

Kannst du die Sprechblasen dem richtigen Bild zuordnen? Verbindet sie mit einer Linie.

A

B

Mei-Lin: *My dad is a great cook. He makes the best Chinese food! His rice with chicken, egg and vegetables is so good!*

Sarah: *For Hanukkah, my grandma makes these amazing latkes. You make them with potatoes, and we eat them with apple sauce.*

E-postcard from the USA

Lies den Text, den Lea über das Essen in den USA schreibt. Was bedeutet hier das Wort ‚tip'in der letzten Zeile auf Deutsch?

Hi, everyone!

The food here is amazing!
I think my favourite is Mexican food. I love tacos!

In American restaurants, you often get free water. And when you pay for your meal, it's very important to give some extra money. That's a 'tip'.

Das englische Wort „tip" bedeutet hier: _____

Partner page

 7 Getting ready ▶ Page 110

a) *Partner/in B: Höre Partner/in A zu. Lies dann vor, was Nish getan hat.*

> I haven't found any nice clothes for the wedding.
> I haven't bought a present for Mum and Ben.
> But I've invited my friends.

b) *Nish und Sunita haben beide eine Sache schon getan. Welche?*

They have _____ their

_____.

Extra practice

Extra practice 1 ▶ page 102

Write the words under the pictures.
Schreibe die Wörter aus der Box unter die passenden Bilder.

- a bonfire
- costumes
- decorations
- fireworks
- ~~a parade~~
- a present

a parade _____ _____

_____ _____ _____

Extra practice 2 ▶ page 105

a) **Look at the pictures and write about the dishes. Use the words in the box.**
Sieh dir die Bilder an und schreibe über die Gerichte. Nutze die Wörter in der Box.

bread • peas • potatoes • sauce • tomatoes

A This is a curry with p *e a s* (1) and

p _ _ _ _ _ _ _ (2) in it. You make the

s _ _ _ _ (3) with t _ _ _ _ _ _ _ (4).

Eat it with rice or b _ _ _ _ (5).

chicken • lemon • oil • pepper • salad

B You make this c_ _ _ _ _ _ (6) with

some l _ _ _ _ (7). It's great

with a green s _ _ _ _ (8) with some

o _ _ (9) and salt and p _ _ _ _ _ (10).

b) **Write about food. Use Wordbank 7 on page 166. Tell each other.**
Schreibe zum Thema Essen. Nutze die Wordbank 7 auf Seite 166. Erzählt es einander.

I often eat _____.

I don't eat _____.

My favourite food is _____.

I don't like _____.

I've never tried _____.

I'm allergic to _____.

▶ Wordbank 7, p. 166

Extra practice 3 ▶ page 105

(Circle) the wrong word. *Umkreise das Wort, das nicht passt.*

1   ice cream / trifle / (pasta)
2   peas / lemonade / tomatoes
3   rice / lamb / chicken

4   fruit / milk / cola
5   melon / sausages / strawberries
6   carrots / cheese / cream

Extra practice 4 ▶ page 106

Look at the picture. Complete Scout's sentences with *some* or *any*.

Sieh dir das Bild an. Ergänze Scouts Sätze mit some *oder* any.

1   Can I have _____ orange juice?

2   I'd like _____ strawberries.

3   I don't want _____ cheese.

4   I'd like _____ cake, please.

5   I don't want _____ salad.

Are you hungry?
What would you like?

Extra practice 5 ▶ page 106

Some or *any*? (Circle) the correct word.

Some oder any? *Umkreise das richtige Wort.*

Dad _____   Let's start a shopping list for the supermarket. What do we have?

Lin _____   We don't have some / any onions. We have some / any peppers, but we
don't have some / any potatoes.

Dad _____   I ate the last banana, so we don't have some / any bananas.

Lin _____   That's right. And we have some / any strawberries, but we don't have
some / any apples.

Dad _____   OK, great! Let's go to the supermarket.

Extra practice 6 ▶ page 109

Read and listen. Say the words.

Lies und höre zu. Sprich die Wörter laut.

be – was – been
see – saw –seen
come – came – come
do – did – done
buy – bought – bought
think – thought – thought
cut[1] – cut – cut
put – put – put

Extra practice 7 ▶ page 109

a) *Deine Lehrkraft hat ein paar Sätze aufgeschrieben und an die Wand gehängt. Partner/in A: Laufe zu einem Satz. Versuche ihn dir vollständig zu merken. Laufe zurück zu Partner/in B. Sage Partner/in B den Satz. Partner/in B: Schreibe den Satz auf ein Blatt Papier. Wechselt euch ab.*

That's a cool activity!

b) *Schneidet eure Sätze in einzelne Papierstreifen. Setzt die Sätze in die richtige Reihenfolge, damit sie einen Dialog ergeben. Übt den Dialog frei zu sprechen.*

Extra practice 8 ▶ page 109

Match. Draw lines. *Ordne zu. Ziehe Linien.*

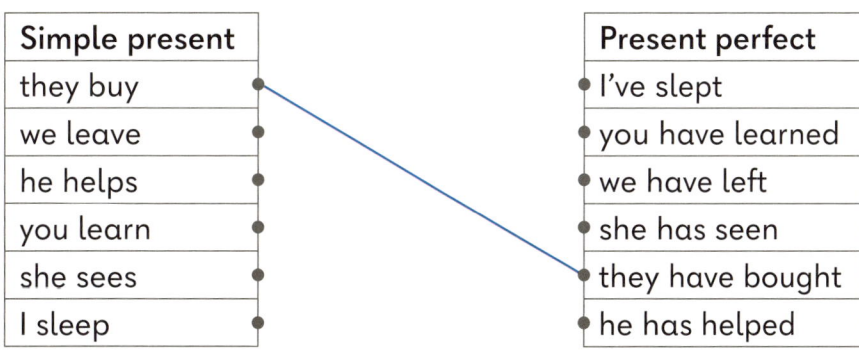

Simple present	Present perfect
they buy	I've slept
we leave	you have learned
he helps	we have left
you learn	she has seen
she sees	they have bought
I sleep	he has helped

---

[1] **cut** *schneiden*

Extra practice 9

▶ page 111

Listen and sing. *Höre zu und singe mit.*

Have you ever, ever, ever in your long-legged life
seen a long-legged sailor with a long-legged wife?
– No, I've never, never, never in my long-legged life,
Seen a long-legged sailor with a long-legged wife.

Extra practice 10

▶ page 113

Read Scout's sentences and (circle) the correct words.
Lies Scouts Sätze und umkreise die richtigen Wörter.

I didn't want to do anything / everywhere (1) today,

but then I remembered: I have a party to

go to tonight! It's going to be a very big party,

everywhere / everyone (2) is going to be there!

Someone / Anything (3) special is going to be there.

But I have a problem. I can't find the present that

I bought, and I've looked someone / everywhere (4) for it.

Extra practice 11

▶ page 116

Write the words under the pictures.
Schreibe die Wörter unter die Bilder.

dress • shoes • slippers • suit • tie

_ _ _ _ _ _ _ _ _ _ _ _ _ _ _ _ _ _ _ _ _ _ _ _

Unit 4

Celebrate!

▶ p. 102	important	wichtig
	bonfire	das (große Freuden-)Feuer
▶ p. 103	fireworks (pl)	das Feuerwerk

| | celebration | die Feier, das Fest |
| | Christmas | Weihnachten |

Topic 1

▶ p. 104	(to) fast	fasten
	(to) celebrate	feiern
	sure	sicher
	tonight	heute Nacht, heute Abend
	everyone	jeder, alle
	meal	die Mahlzeit, das Essen
▶ p. 105	curry	das Curry (Gewürz und auch Gericht)
	juice	der Saft

orange juice

	lamb	das Lamm(fleisch)
	pork	das Schweinefleisch
▶ p. 106	Would you like ...?	Möchtest du ...?
▶ p. 107	of course	natürlich, selbstverständlich
	(to) enjoy	genießen
	Enjoy your meal!	GutenAppetit!
	(to) invite (to)	einladen (zu, nach)

Topic 2

▶ p. 108	wedding	die Hochzeit
	surprise	die Überraschung
	presentation	das Referat, die Präsentation
	she has asked	sie hat gefragt

	(to) think: **she has thought**	sie hat gedacht
	(to) find: **she has found**	sie hat gefunden
	she hasn't ...	sie hat nicht ...
▶ p. 109	**just**	gerade, soeben
	(to) have: **I've had**	ich habe gehabt
	(to) **lose, lost, lost**	verlieren
	(to) **blow, blew, blown**	blasen, pusten
▶ p. 110	(to) **buy: I've bought**	ich habe gekauft
	(to) give: **they have given**	sie haben gegeben
	(to) see: **I've seen**	ich habe gesehen
	(to) **sleep, slept, slept**	schlafen
	(to) **finish**	enden; beenden, zu Ende machen
	(to) **arrive**	ankommen
	(to) get: **they've got here**	sie sind hier angekommen
	(to) come: **she has come**	sie ist gekommen
	full (of ...)	voll; voller ...
▶ p. 111	(to) make: **you've made**	du hast gemacht
	(to) **smile**	lächeln
	(to) be: **I've been**	ich bin gewesen
	(to) eat: **I've eaten**	ich habe gegessen
	(to) tell: **I've told**	ich habe erzählt

Topic 3

▶ p. 113	**someone**	jemand
	amazing	erstaunlich; großartig
	(to) **fly, flew, flown**	fliegen
	onto	auf (etwas hinauf)
	table	der Tisch

	costume	das Kostüm, die Verkleidung

Story

▶ p. 114	(to) **worry**	sich Sorgen machen
	(to) wear: **I've worn**	ich habe getragen
	suit	der (Herren-)Anzug; das (Damen-) Kostüm

suits

▶ p. 115	**just**	nur, bloß
	out	heraus, hinaus, nach draußen
	(to) leave: **they've left**	sie haben verlassen
	(to) **close**	schließen, zumachen
	slippers *(pl)*	die Hausschuhe

	(to) **laugh**	lachen
	(to) **marry**	heiraten
▶ p. 116	**left**	links; nach links
	right	rechts; nach rechts
	on the left/right	auf der linken/rechten Seite

Study skills

| ▶ p. 118 | (to) **speak, spoke, spoken** | sprechen |
| | **mirror** | der Spiegel |

Unit task

| ▶ p. 119 | (to) **put: you've put** | du hast gesetzt |

Unit 5
Getting ready for the future

A

This person makes websites.

B

This person cuts hair.

C

This person stops fires. *1*

D

This person helps ill people.

1 Listening **After the year 8 assembly**

a) Before you listen *Bei der Schulversammlung sprachen ein paar Eltern über ihre Berufe. Sieh dir die Fotos an und lies die Sätze. Ordne die Berufe in der Tabelle den Fotos zu. Schreibe A–H. Vergleicht eure Ergebnisse.*

artist	*H*	builder	___	cook	___	firefighter	___
hairdresser	___	mechanic	___	nurse	___	programmer	___

b) *Höre zu. Bringe die Fotos in die richtige Reihenfolge. Schreibe 1–8 in die Fotos.*

○ über verschiedene Berufe sprechen
○ meine Zukunft beschreiben
○ über Arbeiten im Haushalt reden
○ über Geld und Einkaufen reden
○ geschriebene Texte überprüfen

Unit task ✓

○ Spaß-Horoskope schreiben

This person makes buildings.

This person works on cars.

This person makes food.

This person makes art.

2 My friends' and family's jobs

 a) *Wen kennst du mit diesen Berufen? Schreibe es auf. Erzählt es dann einander.*

> Always use *a* or *an* with jobs:
> My cousin is *a* builder.
> My mum is *an* artist.

I know a / an _____ . My _____

is a / an _____ . I don't know any _____ .

b) *Bildet Gruppen. Eine Person spielt einen Beruf vor. Die anderen raten.*

| Are you a / an ...? | No, that's wrong. | Yes, that's right! |

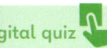 igital quiz **Ich kann** über Berufe sprechen. ✓

Future jobs and plans

1 Reading **Then and now**

a) Before you read *Die Kinder sprechen mit ihrer Freundin Ava über Berufe. Was glaubst du möchten die Kinder werden? Erzählt es einander. Lest dann das Gespräch. Überprüft, ob ihr Recht hattet.*

I think Sunita / Lily / Zane / Noah wants to be a cook / firefighter / programmer / vet.

Lily	What did you want to be when you were little, Ava?
Ava	I wanted to be a nurse. But now I think that maybe I want to work for an animal charity. What about you, Lily?
Lily	I think that I want to be a firefighter. Noah, tell us about you!
Noah	I want to be a vet because I love animals.
Sunita	That's true, but it's a lot of work too – ask my mum! I want to be a gamer, so I can play games all day. And you, Zane?
Zane	When I was little, I wanted to be a footballer. Now I want to be a cook.

b) **Read the text again. Make sentences. Draw lines.**
Lies den Text noch einmal. Bilde Sätze. Ziehe Linien.

1 Ava wants to	2 Lily wants to	3 Noah wants to	4 Sunita wants to	5 Zane wants to
a be a firefighter.	b be a gamer.	c be a vet.	d be a cook.	e work for an animal charity.

▶ Extra practice 1–2, pp.152–153

2 Words **Secret sentences**

a) *Schreibe die Satzanfänge auf ein Blatt Papier und ergänze sie. Nutze die Berufe auf den Seiten 132–133 und die Wordbank 9 auf Seite 168.*

When I was little, I wanted to be a / an ... Now I want to be a / an ...

b) *Eure Lehrkraft sammelt alle Zettel ein und liest einen Satz vor. Wer hat den Satz geschrieben?*

3 Song Hey, world!

a) Before you listen **Write the correct jobs under the pictures.**
Schreibe die richtigen Berufe unter die Bilder.

firefighter • star • vet • writer

1	2	3	4
_____	_____	_____	_____

b) **Listen and complete the song with the jobs in a).** *Höre zu und ergänze im Lied die fehlenden Berufe aus a).*

c) **Listen to the song again. Tick (✓) the best new title for the song.** *Höre das Lied noch einmal. Mache ein Häkchen (✓) neben den Titel, der am besten passt.*

1 I know what I want to be ☐
2 I can do many things ☐
3 I'm scared about my future ☐

Good to know

Im Englischen enden viele Berufe auf *-er*:
sing ▸ singer   write ▸ writer

In der englischen Sprache benutzt du für Berufe von Männern und Frauen häufig dasselbe Wort:
She's a firefighter. He's a firefighter.

Hey, world!

In the future maybe I'll be a
_____.

My friends, they won't believe it

when I'm a famous _____.

Maybe I'll be a _____!

If I work hard, I'll go far.

Or maybe I'll be a _____.

I haven't made my mind up yet.

Erklär-
film

4 Looking at language **The will-future**

a) *Höre das Lied von 3 noch einmal an. Hebe deine Hand wenn du 'll oder won't hörst.*

b) *Unterstreiche 'll und won't im Lied aus Übung 3. Unterstreiche dann 'll und will in Scouts Sprechblase unten. Wähle danach die richtige Antwort in der linken Box (A oder B).*

Wofür verwendest du das *will*-Futur?

A Um zu sagen, was wahrscheinlich in der Zukunft geschehen wird.

B Um zu sagen, was in der Vergangenheit passiert ist.

Du bildest das *will*-Futur mit *will* oder der Kurzform *'ll* und dem Verb (z.B. *be, go*).
Wenn du sagen möchtest, was nicht geschehen wird, verwendest du *won't* (= *will not*).

I'll be a famous singer! George will be my biggest fan! And Black Bird will be my manager!

▶ Extra practice 3, p. 153

5 Crazy predictions

a) **Complete the sentences for your partner.**
Ergänze die Sätze für deinen Partner / deine Partnerin.

1 You'll be a _____ .

a job *(builder, cook, …)*

2 You'll get _____ euros an hour.

a number *(15, 50, …)*

3 You won't work on _____ .

a day of the week *(Sunday, Monday, …)*

4 Your boss will be _____ .

a person *(your teacher, Scout, …)*

b) **Read your sentences from a) to each other. Who has the funnier prediction?**
Lest euch eure Sätze aus a) vor. Wer hat die lustigere Vorhersage?

▶ Extra practice 4, p. 153

6 Reading Finn's poster

Complete Finn's poster about his dream future. *Use 'll or won't.*
Ergänze Finns Poster über seine Traumzukunft. Nutze 'll oder won't.

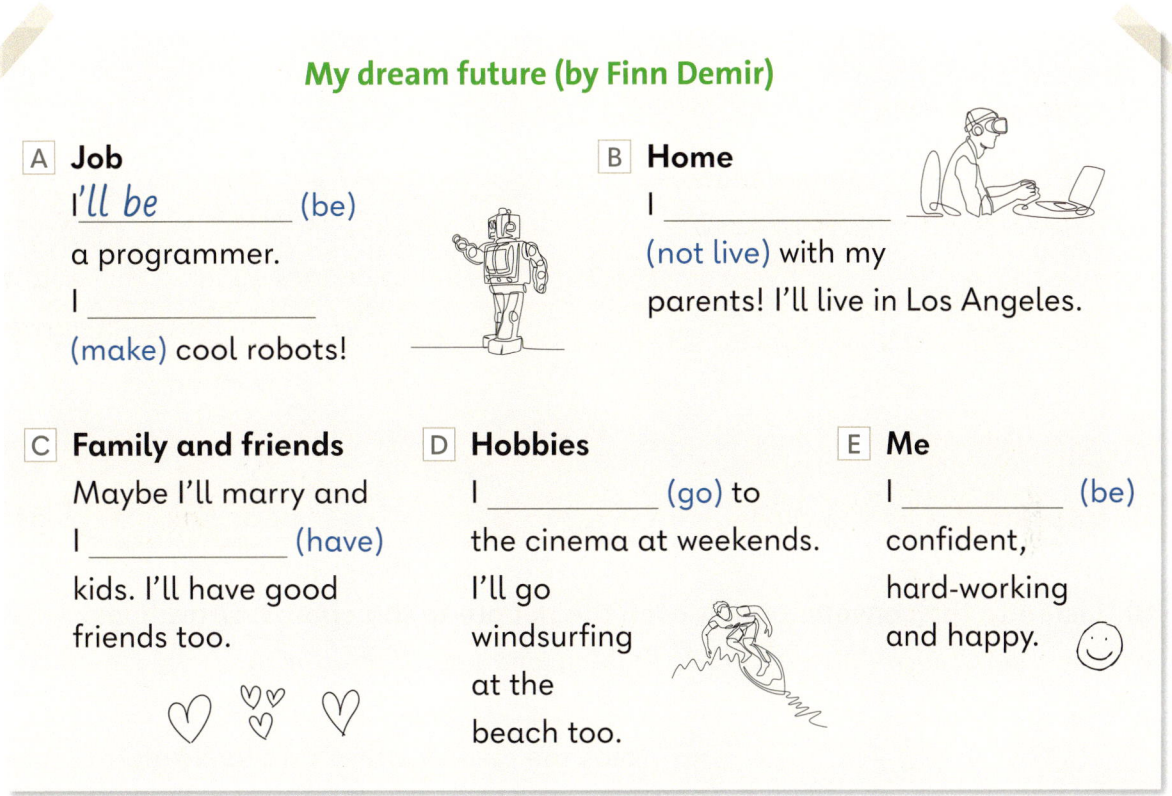

My dream future (by Finn Demir)

A **Job**
I *'ll be* _____ (be)
a programmer.
I _____
(make) cool robots!

B **Home**
I _____
(not live) with my
parents! I'll live in Los Angeles.

C **Family and friends**
Maybe I'll marry and
I _____ (have)
kids. I'll have good
friends too.

D **Hobbies**
I _____ (go) to
the cinema at weekends.
I'll go
windsurfing
at the
beach too.

E **Me**
I _____ (be)
confident,
hard-working
and happy.

My task

7 A poster about my dream future ▶ Digital help

Mache ein Poster über deine Traumzukunft wie in 6. Schreibe Sätze. Hier sind ein paar Ideen. Zeichne Bilder dazu.

	be	a football trainer / a firefighter / a cook / an artist / …
	live	alone / in a big flat / in London / with my friends / …
I'll I won't	have	a partner / kids / pets / friends / …
	go	on holiday / swimming / dancing / to football games / …
	be	brave / happy / hard-working / confident / …

Jobs at home

1 Listening **Look at this room!**

a) Before you listen **Look at the picture. What can you see? Write, then tell each other.**
Sieh dir das Bild an. Was siehst du? Schreibe es auf. Erzählt es dann einander.

I can see *a bed,* _____

b) Listen to the conversation. Match the people to the chores. Draw lines.
Höre dem Gespräch zu. Ordne die Menschen den Arbeiten zu. Ziehe Linien.

1 Nish		a	folds the clean clothes and looks after George.
2 Mum		b	does the washing.
3 Sunita		c	takes out the rubbish and cleans the bathroom.
4 Ben		d	does the shopping and works in the garden.

2 Words **More chores**

Complete the chores under the pictures.
Ergänze die Arbeiten unter den Bildern.

bed • dishwasher • floors • table

set the
_____

empty the
_____

vacuum the
_____

make the
_____

▶ Extra practice 5, p. 154

3 Speaking Chores in class 8C

a) *Sieh dir die Tabelle an. Was zeigt sie?*
Umkreise A oder B.

A It shows the subjects of students.

B It shows what students do at home.

Students in class 8C	Chores
29	make the bed
19	set the table
1	vacuum the floors

b) *Sieh dir die Tabelle in a) noch einmal an.*
Es gibt 30 Kinder in der Klasse 8C. Was müssen die Kinder zu Hause tun, was nicht?
Ergänze die Sätze.

1 29 students have to make their bed.

2 19 students have to set the table.

3 1 student has to _____

_____.

1 student doesn't have to make his/her

_____.

11 students don't have to _____.

_____ students don't have to vacuum

the floors.

4 Scout's chores

Was sagt Scout? Was muss sie machen (✓), was muss sie nicht machen (✗)?
Sieh dir die Liste rechts an. Verbinde.

1 I have to	make dinner.
2 I have to	find food.
3 I don't have to	tidy my home.
4 I don't have to	go to the supermarket.

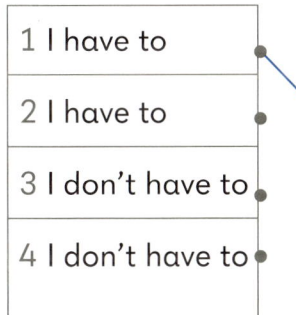

tidy[1] my home ✓
find food ✓
go to the
supermarket ✗
make dinner ✗

▶ Extra practice 6, p. 154

My task

5 My chores

▶ Digital help

Schreibe zwei Sätze in dein Heft über Arbeiten, die du zu Hause machen musst.
Schreibe zwei Sätze über Arbeiten, die du nicht machen musst.

I have to ... I don't have to ...

▶ Wordbank 10, p. 169

---

[1] **tidy** *aufräumen*

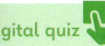

Spend or save?

1 Reading **UK kids and money**

 **a)** Before you read *Bekommst du manchmal Geld oder andere Belohnungen? Sieh dir die Box an. Schreibe es auf. Erzählt es einander.*

I _____

_____

Ideas
- get birthday money
- sell[1] old things
- do chores
- get pocket money[2]
- get extra screen time
- get a film night

b) **Read the article.** *Lies den Artikel.*

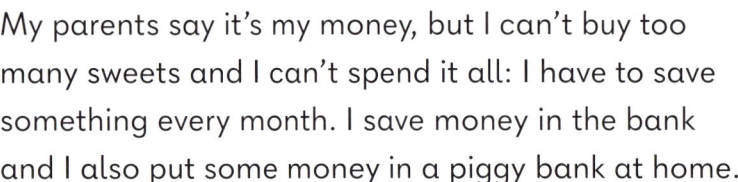

www.pocket-money-uk.example.com

Molly's money (14)
My parents give me pocket money every month.
I buy a lot of clothes. When they're too small, I sell them. I also spend money on books and swimming and going to cafes with my friends.

My parents say it's my money, but I can't buy too many sweets and I can't spend it all: I have to save something every month. I save money in the bank and I also put some money in a piggy bank at home.

Sources: https://roostermoney.com/pocket-money-index-uk (10.11.2022)
https://thefintechtimes.com/61-of-uk-children-use-an-app-to-manage-pocket-money (10.11.22)

c) **True (✓) or false (✗)?** *Wahr (✓) oder unwahr (✗)?*

1 Molly gets pocket money from her parents every week.	✗
2 She sells clothes when they're too small.	
3 She spends money on going to films with friends.	
4 Molly's parents don't want her to spend a lot on sweets.	
5 Molly saves her money in a piggy bank.	

▶ Extra practice 7, p. 155

¹ **sell** *verkaufen*   ² **pocket money** *Taschengeld*

2 Speaking **Your money**

a) **What do you do with your money? Complete the sentences.** *Was machst du mit deinem Geld? Ergänze die Sätze.*

> clothes • online games • …

1 I spend money on _____ .

> in a piggy bank • in a bank • …

2 I save money _____ .

> burgers and chips • sweets • …

3 I can't spend too much money on _____ .

 b) **Tell each other.** *Tauscht euch aus.*

3 Words **Shops and shopping**

a) *Lies den Tipp. Wie heißen die Geschäfte für die Sachen in der Box?*

> bikes • books • pets • toys • sweets

You buy shoes at a shoe shop.
You buy fish and chips at a
fish and chip shop.

b) *Schreibe die Wörter unter die Bilder.*

> old things • sweatshirts • small presents

You can try on

_____

at a clothes shop.

You can find

_____

at a gift[1] shop.

You can give

_____

to a charity shop.

---

[1] **gift** *Geschenk*

4 Viewing **Shopping**

a) Before you watch Read Scout's speech bubble. Say the prices. Take turns.
Lest Scouts Sprechblase. Lest die Preise vor. Wechselt euch ab.

1 £9.99   2 32p   3 £12.95   4 £6.75

> *That donut is sixty-five pence – or sixty-five 'p'. And that sandwich is two pounds twenty.*

b) Watch the video. What does Theo buy? Tick (✓).
Sieh das Video an. Was kauft Theo? Hake ab (✓).

shoes ☐   a T-shirt ☐   a sweatshirt ☐

c) Put sentences A–D in the right order. Watch the video again. Check. *Bringe die Sätze A–D in die richtige Reihenfolge. Sieh das Video noch einmal an. Überprüfe.*

A	Can I help you?	1	A	C	That one is £8.	☐	☐
B	How much is it?	☐	☐	D	Thanks, I'm just looking.	☐	☐

d) Who says what? Write *C* for customer or *A* for assistant next to each number in c).
Wer sagt was? Schreibe C für „customer" (Kunde/Kundin) und A für „assistant" (Verkäufer/Verkäuferin) neben die Nummem in c).

5 That T-shirt is too big

Lies den Tipp. Sieh dir die Bilder A und B an. Umkreise die richtigen blauen Wörter.

this – these
Wenn eine Sache nah ist, verwenden wir „*this*" (Einzahl) oder „*these*" (Mehrzahl).

that – those
Wenn eine Sache weiter weg ist, verwenden wir „*that*" (Einzahl) oder „*those*" (Mehrzahl).

▶ Extra practice 8, p.155

> (This)/ That T-shirt is your size.
> These / Those shoes are £15.

> This / That T-shirt is too big.
> These / Those shoes are £30.

6 Mediation and Speaking **In a gift shop**

a) **Finn is helping a German tourist in a shop in Brighton. Complete the sentences.**
Finn hilft einer deutschen Touristin in einem Laden in Brighton. Ergänze die Sätze.

Tourist	Haben Sie dieses T-Shirt in S?
Finn	Do you have this T-shirt in S?
Assistant	We only have this T-shirt in M and L.
Finn	Sie haben *das T-Shirt* _____ .
Tourist	Dann nehme ich es in M. Was kostet das?
Finn	She wants it in M. How much is it?
Assistant	It's £14.99.
Finn	Es _____ .
Assistant	Would you like to buy a bag? It's 25p.
Finn	Möchten Sie _____ .
Tourist	Ja, bitte.
Finn	She'd like to buy a bag, please.
Assistant	OK. Then it's £15.24.

b) Speaking **Work in a group of three. Read the conversation in a).**
Arbeitet zu dritt. Lest das Gespräch in a). ▶ Extra practice 9, p.156

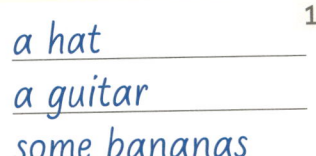

My task

7 Game **Buy and sell**

a) *Bildet zwei Gruppen: „Sellers" (Verkaufende) und „Buyers" (Kaufende).*
Sellers: *Seht euch* Seite 152 *an.*
Buyers: *Wählt eine Einkaufsliste rechts.*

b) Walk around *Du hast £30. Um zu gewinnen,*
musst du alles auf deiner Liste kaufen und am Ende
das meiste Restgeld haben. Nutze diese Redemittel:

Hello. Do you have ...?
How much is it? / How much are they?
Sorry, that's too expensive. I'll give you ...
OK, I'll take it. / OK, I'll take them.

1
a hat
a guitar
some bananas

2
a swimsuit
a robot
some headphones

Goodbye, everybody!

1   Reading   **Ava's great idea**

a)   **Before you read**   **Look at the photos. Answer** question 1. **Then** circle **the correct word in** 2. *Sieh die Fotos an. Beantworte Frage 1. Umkreise dann das richtige Wort in 2.*

    1   Who can you see? I can see _____ .

    2   They are *eating / selling / making* cupcakes.

b)   **Read the story. Check your ideas from** a)**.**
    Lies die Geschichte. Überprüfe deine Antworten in a).

1   Ava wants to make money for an animal charity. But what can she do? She's creative and good at listening. She's good at baking, too, so she wants to sell cupcakes. She asks Zane to help her.

2   On Saturday Ava's dad takes her to the park. Sunita helps Ava to sell the cupcakes. A friendly woman in a blue dress buys two.

3   After an hour Ava has already sold a lot of cupcakes. Her dad is bringing some more, but he's late, so Ava calls him.

4   Finn comes to say goodbye. He says that he's sad to leave his Brighton friends. Sunita is sad too.

> *Hi Dad. When will you be here?*

> *What? I can't hear you. Can you say that again?*

> *OK, Dad. See you soon!*

5 Lily's dad has a new job in London. Her family has to move. Lily is feeling sad. Ava gives Lily a big hug.

6 Sunita and Lily say goodbye. They will miss each other too. Ava has an idea: Sunita can visit Lily in London.

7 Ava's dad has come back with more cupcakes. Just then Zane arrives at the park. Ava gives him a cupcake to say thank you.

8 Noah is unhappy. His parents go everywhere with him! Ava tells him her parents worry about her too.

9 The woman in the blue dress buys ten more cupcakes and gives Ava £100! She tells Ava that she has a bakery. She asks Ava to call her.

10 Ava and her friends have sold all the cupcakes. Now they have £137.20 for the animal charity! It's time to say goodbye. What will happen next?

2 The students in the story

a) *Um wen geht es? Schreibe* Ava, Finn, Lily, Noah *oder* Zane.

1 _Lily_ has to move to a new city.   4 _____ enjoyed helping a friend.

2 _____ wants to do things alone.   5 _____ wants to help a charity.

3 _____ has to go back home.   6 _____ will miss two good friends.

b) *Ergänze Avas Telefonat mit ihrem Vater. Sieh dir Bild 3 auf Seite 144 an.*

Ava ___ Hi Dad. _____ will you be here?
Dad ___ In about five minutes.
Ava ___ What? I can't _____ you.
        Can you say that _____?
Dad ___ I'll be there in five minutes, Ava.
Ava ___ OK, Dad. See you _____!

again • hear • soon • When

▶ Extra practice 10, p.156

3 What will they do?

Make predictions about the students. Draw lines.

Mache Vorhersagen über die Kinder. Ziehe Linien.

1 I think Sunita and Finn will	•	•	talk to his parents.
2 And Lily will	•	•	email each other.
3 I think Noah will	•	•	feel good at her new school.

4 Life skills **Know your strengths**

Ava is creative, good at listening and baking. What about you? Write. *Ava ist kreativ, kann gut zuhören und backen. Was kannst du gut? Schreibe es auf.*

▶ Wordbank 2, p. 161

I'm	brave / clever / fair / friendly / funny / helpful / kind / …
I'm good at	computer games / cooking / dancing / drawing / football / singing / telling jokes / …

Digital quiz 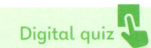 **Ich kann** mich über persönliche Stärken austauschen.

Brighton stories: Chores

1 Emir's chores

Before you watch *Gloria, Daisy und Joe möchten mit Emir einem Marathon zusehen. Emir muss davor seine Haushaltspflichten erledigen. Was glaubst du muss er tun? Hake ab (✓).*

1 wash the dishes[1] ☐   2 fold the clean clothes ☐

3 dry the dishes ☐   3 take out the rubbish ☐

2 Viewing **Help with chores**

a) *Sieh dir das Video an. Welche Haushaltsarbeiten muss Emir erledigen? Überprüfe deine Antwort in 1.*

He has to ...

b) *Sieh dir das Video noch einmal an. Wer erledigt die Haushaltsaufgaben? Umkreise die richtige Antwort.*

1 Gloria und Joe   2 Emir   3 Emir and Joe   4 Daisy and Joe

c) *Was denkt Emir wäre noch eine gute Idee? Umkreise.*

1 clean the bathroom   2 do his homework   3 make his bed   4 tidy his room

3 My opinion

Daisy, Emir, Gloria und Joe sind in drei Wettbewerben gegeneinander angetreten: Holiday experiences *(S. 27),* Street dancing *(S. 57) und* Chores *(diese Seite). Welcher Wettbewerb gefiel euch am besten? Tauscht euch aus.*

I liked the _____ competition best.

[1] **wash the dishes** *das Geschirr waschen*

Check your writing

1 Use a checklist

Finn ist zurück in Deutschland. Er schreibt an Sunita, aber er macht drei Fehler. Lies die Checkliste und dann Finns Brief. Gegen welche Regeln verstößt Finn bei den blau unterstrichenen Fehlern? Schreibe die passende Regel (1–3) neben die Fehler.

CHECKLISTE

1   Meistens schreibst du englische Wörter klein.
- I hope you can visit me one Day.
- I hope you can visit me one <u>day</u>.

2   Aber *I* schreibst du immer groß.
- And i'm happy to see my friends.
- And <u>I'm</u> happy to see my friends.

3   Den Satzanfang schreibst du immer groß.
- we had a long journey home.
- <u>We</u> had a long journey home.

Hello Sunita
Today I'm very tired.
<u>we</u> had a long journey home. ☐

I'm happy to see my dad. I missed him a lot. And <u>i'm</u> happy to see my friends. ☐

Now I miss my English friends.
I hope[1] you can visit me one <u>Day</u>. ☐
Finn

2 Use linking words

Finn hat sehr kurze Sätze in seinem Brief geschrieben.
Lies den Tipp und umkreise dann das richtige Wort in 1–3.

1   Today I'm very tired *because / so* we had a long journey.

2   I'm happy to see my dad *because / so* I've missed him a lot.

3   Now I miss my English friends *because / so* I hope you can visit me one day.

 Sätze lesen sich leichter, wenn du sie miteinander verbindest. Nutze
because = *weil*
so = *also, daher*

3 Write and check your letter

Lies Sunitas Brief und umkreise die richtigen Wörter. Nutze die Tipps aus 1 und 2.

Dear Finn
Thanks for your letter. I hope your next (visit) / Visit is very soon *because / so* I miss you too. *at / At* the supermarket a German woman asked me a question *because / so* I thought of you! Please write soon, *i / I* want to hear from you! Sunita

---

[1] **hope** *hoffen*

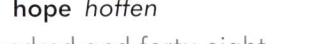 Digital quiz 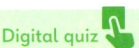   **Ich kann** meine Texte überprüfen. ✓

Write fun horoscopes

Step 1 ▸ Digital help

Was ist dein Sternzeichen? Sieh dir die Tabelle an. Tauscht euch dazu aus.

| CAPRICORN | AQUARIUS | PISCES |
| 22.12. – 19.01. | 20.01. – 18.02. | 19.02. – 20.03. |

| ARIES | TAURUS | GEMINI |
| 21.03. – 19.04. | 20.04. – 20.05. | 21.05. – 20.06. |

| CANCER | LEO | VIRGO |
| 21.06. – 22.07. | 23.07. – 22.08. | 23.08. – 22.09. |

| LIBRA | SCORPIO | SAGITTARIUS |
| 23.09. – 22.10. | 23.10. – 21.11. | 22.11. – 21.12. |

Step 2 ▸ Digital help

a) *Lies diese zwei Vorhersagen.*

You'll have a good day.
You'll learn something interesting.

b) *Schreibe zwei positive Vorhersagen für ein Sternzeichen deiner Wahl auf. Nutze eine Idee aus der Box und eine eigene. Schreibe zuerst für welches Sternzeichen du dich entschieden hast.*

> meet a new person • get a present •
> help a friend • be kind to your family • ...

_____

1 *You'll* _____

2 _____

Step 3 ▸ Digital help

a) *Überprüfe deine Sätze in Step 2b) mit der Checkliste.*

b) *Schreibe deine Sätze auf ein Poster.*

Checkliste
- Hast du die Groß- und Kleinschreibung beachtet?
- Hast du das *will*-Futur richtig benutzt?
- Sind die Vorhersagen positiv?

Step 4

Gallery walk *Lies alle Vorhersagen. Welche gefällt dir?*

1 Words **What do you want to be?**

Ich kann **über Berufe sprechen.**

Some teenagers are talking about their dream jobs. Complete the sentences with the words from the box. *Einige Teenager sprechen über ihre Traumberufe. Ergänze die Sätze mit den Wörtern aus der Box.*

cook • firefighter • hairdresser • mechanic • programmer

Lewis ___ I want to be a _____ (1) because I want to make websites.

Evie ___ That's cool. I love food, so I want to be a _____ (2).

Sam ___ I want do so something with cars – maybe I'll be a _____ (3).

Shakiel _ I like making people look good, so I want to be a _____ (4).

Mia ___ I don't have a dream job. I just know that I want to help people.

Lewis ___ There are lots of jobs for you then! Maybe a _____ (5)?

Mia ___ Maybe!

2 Language **My dream home**

Ich kann **Vorhersagen über die Zukunft machen (*will*-Futur).**

Sunita is writing to Finn about her dream home. Complete the sentences with *will* or *won't*. *Sunita schreibt an Finn über ihr Traumhaus. Ergänze die Sätze mit* will *oder* won't.

---

to   Finn

from   Sunita

My future home ___*will be*___ (1 be) in Brighton,

but it _____ (2 not be) like other houses!

It _____ (3 have) ten bedrooms, a

swimming pool and a cinema. I _____

(4 not leave) my house at the weekend because

all of my friends _____ (5 visit) me.

On Saturdays we _____ (6 swim) in the pool and watch films together,

and then we _____ (7 play) computer games.

Check

3 Speaking **The worst chores!**

a) Match the pictures to the activities. Draw lines.
Ordne die Bilder den Aktivitäten zu. Ziehe Linien.

set the table	make the bed	go to the supermarket	vacuum the floors	empty the dishwasher

b) Who has the worst chores? Why? Tell each other.
Wer hat die schrecklichsten Haushaltspflichten? Warum? Erzählt es einander.

I think Sunita/Noah has the worst chores because she/he has to …

I agree.

I don't agree. That chore is OK.

4 Listening **A shopping trip**

Lily und ihr Vater gehen einkaufen. In welche Geschäfte gehen sie? Höre zu und setze die Bilder in die richtige Reihenfolge. Schreibe 1–4. Es gibt ein Bild zu viel.

gift shop

newsagent's[1]

electronics[2] shop

clothes shop 1

bakery

[1] **newsagent** *Zeitungshändler/in* [1] **electronics** *elektronische Geräte*

Check

Partner page

7 My task **Buy and sell** ▶ page 143

a) Sellers (*Verkaufende*): Wähle eine Karte. Schreibe auf deine Karte, wieviel jede Sache kostet. *Die* Buyers (*Kaufenden*) haben £30.

b) Walk around *Stelle dich an einen Tisch. Die Kaufenden fragen nach bestimmten Sachen. Verkaufe sie ihnen. Um zu gewinnen, verkaufe alles auf deiner Karte und verdiene das meiste Geld. Nutze im Gespräch diese Sätze.*

Sorry, I don't have that. /
Sorry, I don't have those.
Yes, I have that. / Yes, I have those.
It's ... / They're ...
Sorry, that's too little. How about ...?

1
a hat £ ___
a guitar £ ___
some bananas £ ___

2
a swimsuit £ ___
a robot £ ___
some headphones £ ___

Extra practice

Extra practice 1 ▶ page 134

Finde die Berufe aus der Box im Kreuzworträtsel. → *bedeutet waagerecht;* ↓ *bedeutet senkrecht. Umkreise die Wörter im Rätsel.*

E	B	S	C	X		E	H	L	W	C		D	U	H
	P	R	O	G	R	A	M	M	E	R	E	W		R
J	I	T	O	A		L	V	U	T	S	Q	H	B	
Q	D	L	K	M	L	Q		T	S	B	P	A	N	
P	B		U	T	E	R	Z	N	E		D	M	I	G
O	U	N		F		C	Y	W	O	R	C	R		
F	I	R	E	F	I	G	H	T	E	R	W	R	D	B
W	L	M	P	Q	G	W	Y	Z		C	Y	W	R	K
S	D	X		R	Y	S	N	T	E	A	C	H	E	R
M	E	C	H	A	N	I	C	D	X		Y	W	S	M
	R	Z	F	T	U	X		Y	W	E	I	G	S	F
F	Z	E	X	W	R	N	P	V	C	D		V	E	T
J	X		Y	E	S	F	K	S			Y	W	R	C
		R	V	R	E	A		T	W	C	V	G	Y	

→ firefighter
→ mechanic
→ programmer
→ teacher
→ vet

↓ builder
↓ cook
↓ nurse
↓ hairdresser

▶ page 134

Extra practice 2

Match the sentences to the jobs. Draw lines.
Ordne die Sätze den Berufen zu. Ziehe Linien.

1 This person works in a school with students.	a writer
2 This person is famous and can act or sing.	b vet
3 This person writes books or stories.	c teacher
4 This person helps animals when they are ill.	d football trainer
5 This person works in a stadium.	e star

▶ page 136

Extra practice 3

Read the sentences. Match. Draw lines. *Lies die Sätze. Ordne sie zu. Ziehe Linien.*

1 We're bored.	a I won't need a sweatshirt.
2 I'm tired.	b She'll call her friends.
3 It's hot outside.	c We'll play video games.
4 She's feeling sad.	d I'll eat a sandwich.
5 I'm hungry.	e I won't go to the cinema tonight.

▶ page 136

Extra practice 4

Complete Scout's sentences with a verb from the box. The pictures can help you.
Ergänze Scouts Sätze mit einem Verb aus der Box. Die Bilder können dir helfen.

Tomorrow I think I'll _____*walk*_____ (1 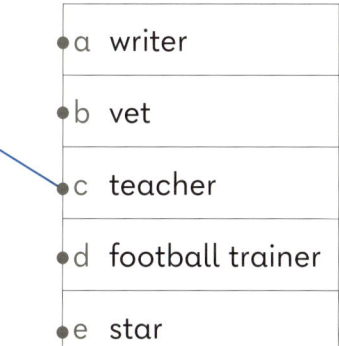) to Hove Beach with Blue Bird and maybe we'll _____ (2) to the street musicians. Then we'll _____ (3) for some lunch. Blue Bird will _____ (4) lots of chips. In the afternoon I won't _____ (5) home because I'll meet Black Bird in the park!

eat • listen • look • ~~walk~~ • walk

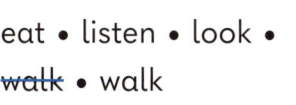

▶ page 138

Extra practice 5

Match the pictures to the activities. Draw lines.

Ordne die Bilder den Aktivitäten zu. Ziehe Linien.

| make dinner | look after a pet | empty the dishwasher | take out the rubbish |

| wash the dishes[1] | fold the clean clothes | set the table | go to the supermarket |

▶ page 139

Extra practice 6

Noahs Familie hat eine Haushalthilfe, Adam.
Was müssen Adam, Noah und seine Eltern tun?
Umkreise die richtigen Wörter in den Sätzen 1–4.

1 Adam has to / doesn't have to vacuum all the floors.

2 Noah's mum and dad have to / don't have to vacuum the floors.

3 Noah's mum and dad have to / don't have to work in the garden.

4 Adam has to / doesn't have to tidy Noah's room.

Adam:
– vacuum all the floors

Noah's mum and dad:
– work in the garden

Noah:
– tidy his room

---

[1] **wash the dishes** *das Geschirr waschen*

▶ page 140

Extra practice 7

Complete the conversation with the words from the box.
Ergänze das Gespräch mit Wörtern aus der Box.

buy • save • sell • spend

Sunita ___ Do you get pocket money, Noah?

Noah ___ Yes, I do. I get £10 every week.

Sunita ___ I only get £5. But I often _____(1) old video games. Then I have more money.

Noah ___ I _____(2) a little money in the bank every month. What about you?

Sunita ___ I'm not good at that! I like to _____(3) things like games and burgers.

Noah ___ I like to _____(4) money on burgers, but my parents don't like that!

▶ page 142

Extra practice 8

⟨Circle⟩ the correct words in blue. *Umkreise die richtigen Wörter in Blau.*

Lily ___ Do you like ⟨these⟩/ those white shoes, Zane?

Zane ___ They're OK. But I like these / those black shoes better.

Lily ___ Yes, they're nice, but I want white ones.

Zane ___ Oh right. Oh, this / that red sweatshirt is cool. I like red – this / that red T-shirt is my favourite.

Lily ___ I like red too. The sweatshirt looks good with these / those yellow trousers.

Zane ___ Mm, I don't like yellow. I like black or blue trousers – or white trousers like these / those ones.

Extra practice 9

▶ page 143

Put the conversation in the right order. Write 1–4. Listen and check.
Setze das Gespräch in die richtige Reihenfolge. Schreibe 1–4. Höre zu und überprüfe.

Assistant ___	Yes, here is size M.	___
Customer ___	OK, I'll take it. Here's £20.	

Assistant ___	Here's your T-shirt. Have a nice day.	___
Customer ___	Thanks, bye!	

Assistant ___	Can I help you?	___
Customer ___	Yes, please. How much is this T-shirt?	

Assistant ___	It's £20.	___
Customer ___	Do you have it in M?	

Extra practice 10

▶ page 146

Ava ruft die Frau aus dem Park an. Lies das Gespräch. Überlege dann, ob die Sätze 1–4 wahr (✓) oder unwahr (✗) sind?

Ms Osman ___	Hello, this is Sara Osman.
Ava ___	Hello, Ms Osman. This is Ava Burt. You gave me your phone number.
Ms Osman ___	Hi Ava. Your cupcakes were great. Do you want to learn more about baking?
Ava ___	Yes, I do!
Ms Osman ___	Can (crr...) bakery (crr...) Tuesday?
Ava ___	Sorry, I can't hear you. Can you say that again please?
Ms Osman ___	I said can you come to my bakery after school on Tuesday?
Ava ___	Yes, I can.
Ms Osman ___	OK. See you then. Bye, Ava. See you soon.
Ava ___	Goodbye.

1 Ms Osman doesn't remember Ava. ☐

2 Ms Osman liked Ava's cupcakes. ☐

3 Ava wants to learn more about baking. ☐

4 Ava will go to the bakery on Thursday. ☐

Unit 5

Getting ready for the future

▶ p. 132	(to) **cut, cut, cut**	schneiden
	fire	das Feuer
	artist	der Künstler, die Künstlerin
	builder	der Bauarbeiter, die Bauarbeiterin; der Bauunternehmer, die Bauunternehmerin
	firefighter	der Feuerwehrmann, die Feuerwehrfrau

a **firefighter** trying to stop a **fire**

	hairdresser	der Friseur, die Friseurin
	mechanic	der Mechaniker, die Mechanikerin
	nurse	der Krankenpfleger. die Krankenpflegerin

nurse

	programmer	der Programmierer, die Programmiererin
▶ p. 133	(to) **work on sth.**	an etwas arbeiten, etwas bearbeiten

Topic 1

▶ p. 134	**maybe**	vielleicht	
	charity	die wohltätige Organisation	
	so	also, daher	
▶ p. 135	**writer**	der Schriftsteller, die Schriftstellerin	
	I'll (= I will) be …	ich werde … sein	
	I won't (= will not) be …	Ich werde nicht … sein	
	famous	berühmt	
	future	die Zukunft	
▶ p. 137	**dream**	der Traum	**My dream future** = meine Traumzukunft

Topic 2

▶ p. 138	(to) **fold**	falten
	clean	sauber
	washing	die Wäsche
	(to) **clean**	sauber machen, putzen
	dishwasher	die Geschirrspülmaschine

The **dishwasher** is finished! Can you **empty** it, please?

	floor	der Fußboden
	(to) **set the table**	den Tisch decken
	(to) **empty**	leeren
	(to) **vacuum**	Staub saugen
▶ p. 139	**chore**	die (Haus-)Arbeit, die *(lästige)* Pflicht
	(to) **have to** do sth.	etwas tun müssen
	(to) **tidy**	aufräumen

Topic 3

▶ p. 140	(to) **sell, sold, sold**	verkaufen
	pocket money	das Taschengeld
	(to) **spend (money on ...)**	(Geld) ausgeben (für ...)
	sweets *(pl)*	die Bonbons, die Süßigkeiten
	(to) **save**	sparen
	piggy bank	das Sparschwein

▶ p. 141	**gift**	das Geschenk
▶ p. 142	**pound (£)**	das Pfund *(britische Währung)*
	penny (p), *pl* **pence**	der Penny, Pence *(Plural)*
	The football is £3. The books are £2.	Der Fußball kostet 3 Pfund. Die Bücher kosten 2 Pfund.
	size	die Größe

	those	die dort, jene (dort)
▶ p. 143	only	nur, bloß; erst

Story

▶ p. 144	creative	kreativ
	(to) bake	backen
	cupcake	der Cupcake (kleiner Muffin-ähnlicher Kuchen)

cupcakes

	woman, *pl* women	die Frau
	(to) call	rufen; anrufen
	(to) leave, left, left	verlassen
▶ p. 145	hug	die Umarmung
	(to) miss	vermissen
	each other	einander, sich (gegenseitig)
	bakery	die Bäckerei

Study skills

▶ p. 148	(to) hope	hoffen
	letter	der Brief

Wordbank 1: Holiday activities

▶ Unit 1 | p. 17

go rafting

go snorkelling

do a treetop walk

ride down a luge track

go windsurfing

water activities

go to a water park

mountain activities

go hiking

go on a zipline

go on a boat ride

go paddleboarding

holiday activities

go mountain biking

have a sleepover

make videos / a playlist

go sightseeing

relax with friends

city activities

watch a parade

paint my room

activities at home

make a cake / ice cream / pizza

go to the cinema

do origami

have a picnic

visit a castle / museum / market

play crazy golf

have a water fight

Wordbank 2: Describing a person

▶ Unit 5 | p. 146

He/She has blond / brown / red / short / long / straight / curly hair, braces, …

a crew cut

gelled hair

a ponytail

a fringe

plaits

a beard

freckles

nail varnish

airbrushed nails

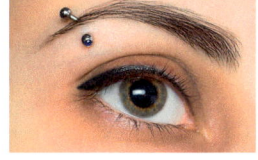
a piercing

a tattoo

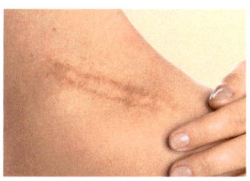
a scar

Skills and activities   He/She is good at maths, sports, listening, drawing, organizing things, solving problems, …
He/She is a good with children, animals, computers, …

Personality

ambitious	*ehrgeizig*	honest	*ehrlich*
artistic	*künstlerisch*	imaginative	*fantasievoll*
brave	*mutig*	independent	*unabhängig*
calm	*ruhig, gelassen*	motivated	*motiviert*
caring	*mitfühlend, fürsorglich*	open-minded	*aufgeschlossen, offen*
cheerful	*fröhlich*	organized	*organisiert*
clever, smart	*klug*	patient	*geduldig*
confident	*selbstbewusst*	practical	*praktisch*
creative	*kreativ*	punctual	*pünktlich*
curious	*neugierig*	reliable	*verlässlich, zuverlässig*
dramatic	*dramatisch*	romantic	*romantisch*
easy-going	*gelassen, locker*	sensitive	*sensibel, empfindsam*
energetic	*energisch, tatkräftig*	shy	*schüchtern*
flexible	*flexibel*	sociable	*kontaktfreudig, gesellig*
hard-working	*fleißig*	strong	*stark*
helpful	*hilfsbereit*	tidy	*ordentlich*

Wordbank 3: Clothes and accessories

▶ Unit 2 | p. 52

cape

coat

jacket

hoodie

jumper

underwear

T-shirt

swimsuit

clothes

shirt

tights

dress

tie

skirt

jeans

socks

trousers

shorts

shoes

trainers

boots

sandals

jewellery

helmet

gloves

sunglasses

accessories

scarf

belt

hat

mask

Wordbank 4: Parts of the body

▶ Unit 2 | p. 56

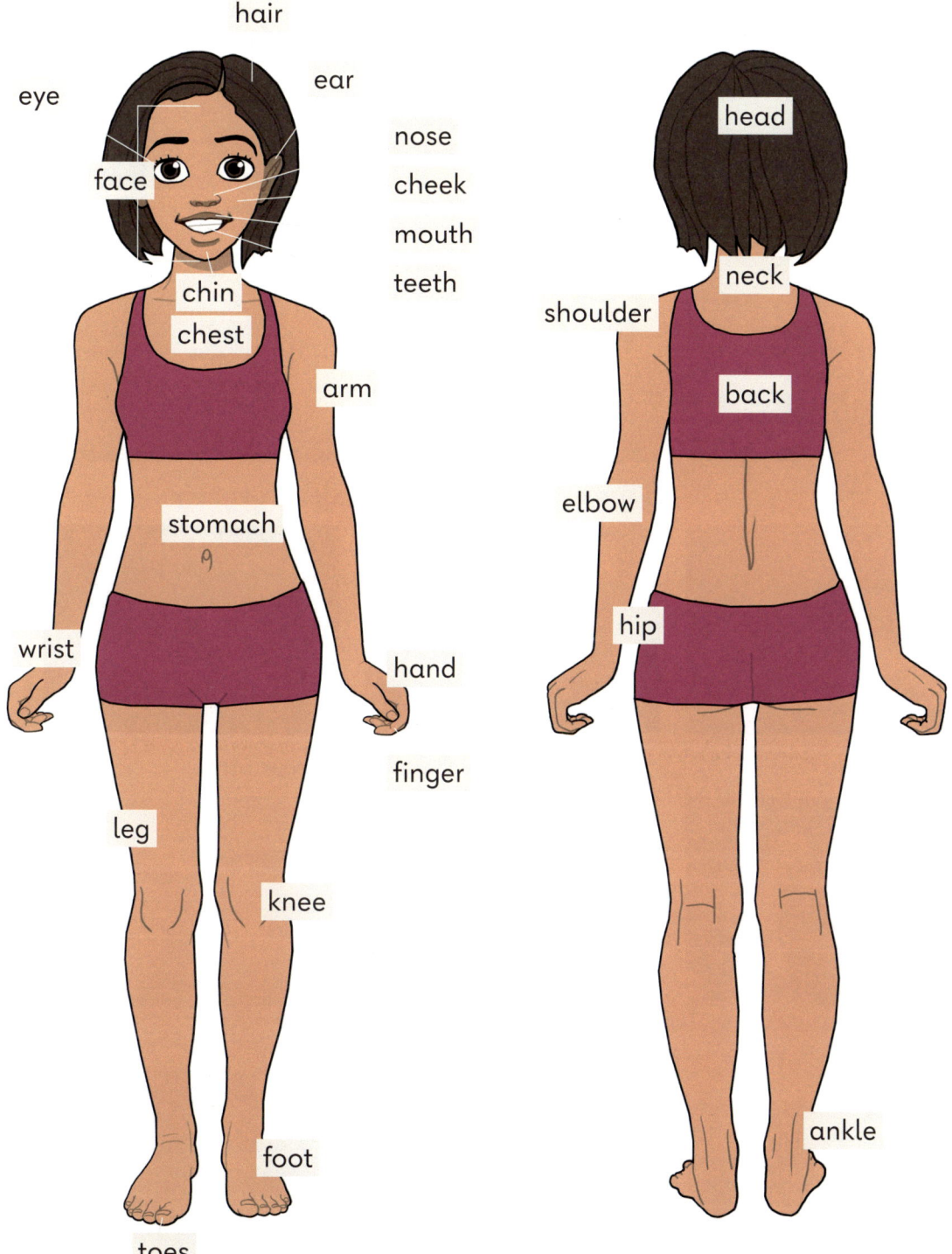

hair
eye
ear
nose
cheek
mouth
teeth
face
chin
chest
arm
stomach
wrist
hand
finger
leg
knee
foot
toes

head
neck
shoulder
back
elbow
hip
ankle

Wordbank 5: Films and shows

▶ Unit 3 | p. 81

action film

cartoon

comedy

cooking show

disaster film

documentary

fantasy film

game show

horror film

reality show

romance

science fiction (sci-fi) film

soap

sports show

thriller

Wordbank 6: Online activities

▶ Unit 3 | p. 84

Social media	**Soziale Medien**
(to) like photos / posts	Fotos / Posts liken
(to) post comments	Kommentare posten
(to) post photos	Fotos posten

Video sharing sites	**Webseiten zum Austausch von Videos**
(to) watch videos for fun	Videos zum Spaß anschauen
(to) watch fitness videos	Fitness-Videos anschauen
and do workouts	und trainieren
(to) upload videos	Videos hochladen

Messaging services	**Messaging-Dienste**
(to) chat	chatten
(to) make new friends	neue Freunde gewinnen
(to) send / read messages	Nachrichten senden / lesen

Gaming and puzzle sites	**Spiel- und Rätselwebseiten**
(to) play multiplayer games	Multiplayer-Spiele spielen
(to) do interactive puzzles	interaktive Spiele spielen

Music sites	**Musik-Webseiten**
(to) listen to music	Musik hören
(to) make playlists	Playlists erstellen

Sites for information and help	**Informations- und Hilfewebseiten**
(to) find the way	den Weg finden
(to) plan routes	Routen planen
(to) look up new words	neue Wörter nachschlagen
(to) check facts	Fakten überprüfen
(to) find photos	Fotos finden
(to) watch online tutorials	Online-Anleitungen anschauen

Other websites	**Andere Webseiten**
(to) take a virtual tour	eine virtuelle Tour machen
(to) listen to podcasts	Podcasts anhören
(to) create stories	Geschichten schreiben
(to) do slideshows	Slideshows erstellen
(to) make short films	Kurzfilme drehen
(to) create animations	Animationen erstellen

Wordbank 7: Food

▶ Unit 4 | pp. 107, 125

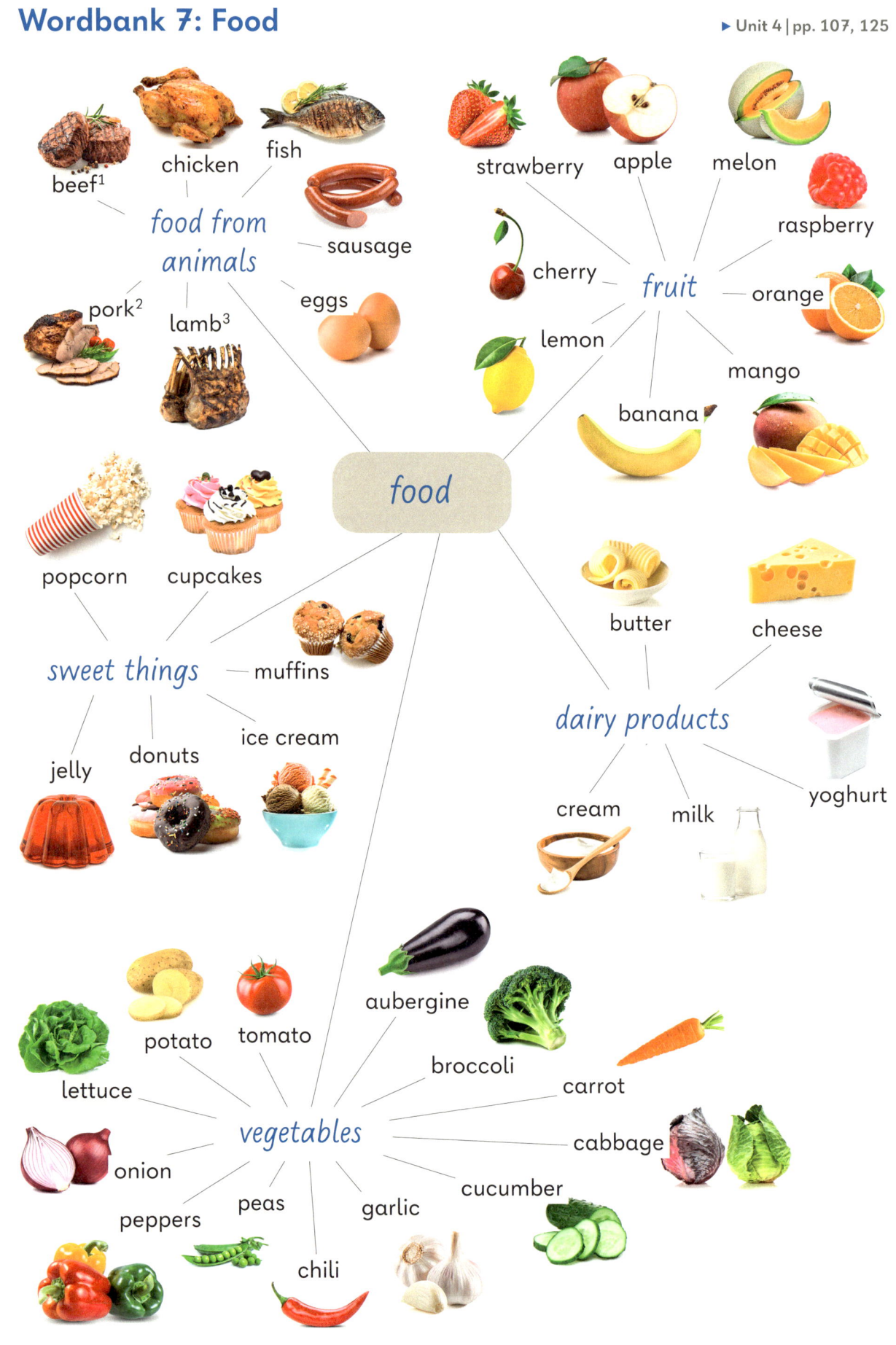

food from animals
- beef[1]
- chicken
- fish
- sausage
- pork[2]
- lamb[3]
- eggs

fruit
- strawberry
- apple
- melon
- raspberry
- cherry
- orange
- lemon
- mango
- banana

food

sweet things
- popcorn
- cupcakes
- muffins
- jelly
- donuts
- ice cream

dairy products
- butter
- cheese
- cream
- milk
- yoghurt

vegetables
- aubergine
- broccoli
- carrot
- potato
- tomato
- lettuce
- cabbage
- cucumber
- onion
- peas
- garlic
- peppers
- chili

[1] **beef** *das Rindfleisch*   [2] **pork** *das Schweinefleisch*   [3] **lamb** *das Lamm; Lammfleisch*

Wordbank 8: Presentations

▶ Unit 4 | pp. 118, 119

Continue the presentation

First ... / Let me start with ...

Next ... / Then ...

Finally ...

Start the presentation

Hello, everyone!

Can everybody hear me?

I'm going to talk about ...

Talk about pictures and videos

Let's look at this picture of ...

In this picture you can see ...

This photo shows ...

Now we're going to show a short video.

End the presentation

That's the end of my presentation.

Thank you for listening.

Do you have any questions?

Explain and correct yourself

This word means ...

Sorry, that's the wrong word. I mean ...

Sorry, I've forgotten the word. It's when ...

Wordbank 9: Jobs and workplaces

▶ Unit 5 | p. 134

My mum / dad / … is a/an …
architect, artist, builder, bus driver, business owner, cook, dancer, firefighter, gamer, footballer, hairdresser, mechanic, nurse, police officer, programmer, teacher, train driver, vet, writer

beautician   call centre agent   care worker   cashier

dentist   electrician   engineer   lawyer

paramedic   plumber   secretary   shop assistant

My mum / dad / … works at / on / in a/an …
cafe, cinema, hospital, library, museum, office, restaurant, school, shop, shopping centre, sports centre, supermarket, train station

in/at a factory   on/at a farm   in/at a garage   in/at a laboratory

My brother / sister / … is unemployed. (He / She doesn't have a job.)
My mum / dad is a full-time parent.

Wordbank 10: Chores

▶ Unit 5 | p. 139

(to) babysit, (to) clean the bathroom, (to) do the washing, (to) empty the dishwasher,
(to) fold the clean clothes, (to) look after the family's pet, (to) make my bed,
(to) set the table, (to) take out the rubbish, (to) tidy my room, (to) vacuum the floors

Cleaning

(to) clean out my pet's cage
den Käfig meines Haustiers saubermachen

(to) do the dusting
Staub wischen

(to) take bottles to the bottle bank *Flaschen zum Container bringen*

(to) take cans / paper / plastic to the recycling containers
Dosen / Papier / Plastik zu den Recyclingcontainern bringen

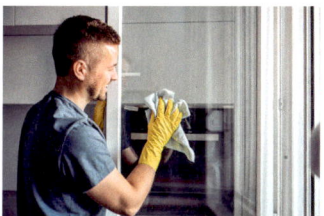

(to) clean the windows
die Fenster putzen

(to) clean my bike
mein Fahrrad putzen

Meals

(to) clear the table
den Tisch abräumen

dry the dishes
abtrocknen

(to) feed pets
die Haustiere füttern

wash up
abwaschen

(to) load the dishwasher
die Spülmaschine einräumen

Clothes

(to) clean my shoes
meine Schuhe putzen

(to) do the ironing
bügeln

(to) hang up the washing
die Wäsche aufhängen

infinitive	simple past	past participle	
(to) **be**	was/were	**been**	*sein*
(to) **become**	became	**become**	*werden*
(to) **blow**	blew	**blown**	*blasen, pusten*
(to) **bring**	brought	**brought**	*(mit)bringen*
(to) **buy**	bought	**bought**	*kaufen*
(to) **choose**	chose	**chosen**	*(aus)wählen*
(to) **come**	came	**come**	*kommen*
(to) **cut**	cut	**cut**	*schneiden*
(to) **do**	did	**done**	*tun*
(to) **draw**	drew	**drawn**	*zeichnen*
(to) **drink**	drank	**drunk**	*trinken*
(to) **eat**	ate	**eaten**	*essen*
(to) **fall**	fell	**fallen**	*fallen*
(to) **feel**	felt	**felt**	*(sich) fühlen*
(to) **fight**	fought	**fought**	*kämpfen*
(to) **find**	found	**found**	*finden*
(to) **fly**	flew	**flown**	*fliegen*
(to) **get**	got	**got**	*bekommen, werden*
(to) **give**	gave	**given**	*geben*
(to) **have**	had	**had**	*haben*
(to) **hear**	heard	**heard**	*hören*
(to) **hurt**	hurt	**hurt**	*schmerzen, wehtun*
(to) **know**	knew	**known**	*wissen; kennen*
(to) **leave**	left	**left**	*verlassen*
(to) **lose**	lost	**lost**	*verlieren*

infinitive	simple past	past participle	
(to) make	made	made	*machen*
(to) meet	met	met	*treffen*
(to) pay	paid	paid	*bezahlen*
(to) put	put	put	*legen, stellen*
(to) read	read	read	*lesen*
(to) ride	rode	ridden	*reiten; (Rad) fahren*
(to) run	ran	run	*rennen*
(to) say	said	said	*sagen*
(to) see	saw	seen	*sehen*
(to) sell	sold	sold	*verkaufen*
(to) send	sent	sent	*senden, schicken*
(to) set the table	set	set	*den Tisch decken*
(to) show	showed	shown	*zeigen*
(to) sing	sang	sung	*singen*
(to) sit	sat	sat	*sitzen, sich setzen*
(to) speak	spoke	spoken	*sprechen*
(to) spend	spent	spent	*(Geld) ausgeben, (Zeit) verbringen*
(to) swim	swam	swum	*schwimmen*
(to) take	took	taken	*nehmen; (Zeit) dauern*
(to) tell	told	told	*erzählen*
(to) think	thought	thought	*denken*
(to) understand	understood	understood	*verstehen*
(to) wear	wore	worn	*tragen, anhaben*
(to) write	wrote	written	*schreiben*

Quellenverzeichnis

Titelbild
Cornelsen/Tauziehen (Bild re.): Anja Poehlmann; Häuschen (Bild li.): Shutterstock.com/JoolsW

Illustrationen
Cornelsen/**Harald Ardeias:** (S. 5 Topic 1; S. 5 Story ; S. 5 Unit Task; S. 6 Topic 2; S. 6 Story; S. 7 Topic 3; S. 7 Story; S. 8 Topic 3; S. 8 Story; S. 9 Topic 3; S. 15 unten; S. 16; S. 18 A–D + unten re.; S. 23 Oben; S. 24–25; S. 29 Mitte; S. 32; S. 37–38; S. 48 oben; S. 49; S. 54/1–3; S. 55/4–7; S. 66 unten re.; S. 68 oben re; S. 68 oben li., S. 74/1; S. 80/A–C; S. 82 Karte; S. 83 unten re.; S. 84 alle; S. 85 alle; S. 91 alle; S. 95 alle; S. 98/1–4; S. 104; S 110 Mitte re.; S. 110 unten re.; S. 111 Mitte; S. 112; S. 114; S. 115 alle; S. 116; S. 120; S. 124 oben re.; S. 125/A+B; S. 128 oben re.; S. 138 oben; S. 142 unten; S. 143 oben re.; S. 155 unten re.; S. 163) Cornelsen/**Carlos Borrell Eiköter**: (Europa-Karte Umschlaginnenseite hinten (U3)); (Cornelsen/**Irina Zinner:** (Möwen: S. 4; S. 5; S. 6; S.7; S. 8; S. 9; S. 10; S. 14; S. 17; S. 19; S. 21; S. 23; S. 26; S. 29; S. 36; S. 45; S. 47; S. 48; S. 50; S. 51; S. 53; S. 59; S. 61; S. 67; S. 76; S. 77, S. 79; S. 81; S. 83; S. 86; S. 89; S. 97 unten re.; S. 106; S. 107; S. 109; S. 110; S. 111; S 118; S. 119; S 126; S. 127; S. 128; S. 136; S. 137; S. 139; S. 142; S. 143; S. 149; S. 153; S. 167; S. 176).

Abbildungen
Umschlaginnenseite vorne (**U2**): bitte siehe unter S. 12, 14 + 24; **S. 1**: bitte siehe unter S. 28, 29, 30, 32, 39, 160; **S. 4** oben: Cornelsen/Anja Poehlmann; **S. 5** Travel and holidays: Shutterstock.com/ Maksim Zaytsev, Topic 2: Cornelsen/Anja Poehlmann, Topic 3: Cornelsen/Junge (li.): Anja Poehlmann, Frau (re.): Shutterstock.com/SpeedKingz; **S. 6** Friends and heroes + Topic 1: Cornelsen/Anja Poehlmann, Topic 3: Cornelsen/Inhouse/Josephine Bienert-Köhler, Unit task: interfoto e.k./Granger, NYC; **S. 7** Activities and games: Shutterstock.com/Ironika, Topic 2: Cornelsen/Anja Poehlmann, Study skills (Junge): stock.adobe.com/pairhandmade, Study skills (Mädchen): Shutterstock.com/ViDI Studio, Unit Task: Shutterstock.com/Duda Vasilii; **S. 8** Celebrate! (Farben): stock.adobe.com/ Katarzyna Leszczynsk, Celebrate! (Essen): stock.adobe.com/Fevziie, Topic 1 + Topic 2: Cornelsen/ Anja Poehlmann, Study skills: Imago Stock & People GmbH/Sylvio Dittrich; **S. 9** Getting ready for the future: Shutterstock.com/Gorodenkoff, Topic 1: Shutterstock.com/Pinkcandy, Story: Cornelsen/Anja Poehlmann, Unit Task: Shutterstock.com/Tom K Photo; **S. 10** Selfie : Cornelsen/Anja Poehlmann, Emoticon: Shutterstock.com/Yefym Turkin; **S. 11**: Cornelsen/Anja Poehlmann, Emoticons: Shutterstock.com/Yefym Turkin; **S. 12**/1: Shutterstock.com/Maksim Zaytsev, 2: Shutterstock.com/Bobo Ling, 3: Shutterstock.com/wavebreakmedia, Mitte.li.: Cornelsen/Anja Poehlmann, Wettersymbole: Shutterstock.com/Laenz; **S. 13**/4: Shutterstock.com/Linda George, 5: Shutterstock.com/A_Lein, 6: Shutterstock.com/malik965, Mitte re.: Cornelsen/Anja Poehlmann; **S. 14** oben re.: Shutterstock.com/ vovidzha; **S. 15** Mitte re.: Cornelsen/Anja Poehlmann; **S. 17** Mitte: Shutterstock.com/Radha Design; **S. 18** oben re.: mauritius images/alamy stock photo/Lloyd Lane; **S. 19** oben re.: Cornelsen/Grasshopper Films; **S. 20** Foto oben + unten: Cornelsen/Anja Poehlmann; Foto Mitte: mauritius images/ alamy stock photo/Benedicte Desrus; Emoticon: Shutterstock.com/Yefym Turkin; Regenbogenfahne: Shutterstock.com/daddy.icon; Kuchen: Shutterstock.com/JosepPerianes; Regenbogen (Mitte): Shutterstock.com/Carboxylase; Gitarre: Shutterstock.com/orbitoclast; Kopfhörer: Shutterstock.com/ M_Videous; **S. 22** oben + Mitte: Cornelsen/Anja Poehlmann, unten: Collage: Cornelsen/Junge (li.): Anja Poehlmann, Frau (re.): Shutterstock.com/SpeedKingz; **S. 27** oben: Cornelsen/Inhouse/Mara Leibowitz; **S. 27** unten: Cornelsen/Grasshopper Films; **S. 30** oben li.: Cornelsen/Anja Poehlmann, 1: Shutterstock.com/Rainer Lesniewski, 2: Shutterstock.com/FotoAndalucia, 3: Shutterstock.com/ Naypong Studio, 4: Shutterstock.com/Laenz, 5: Shutterstock.com/Arsenie Krasnevsky, Emoticon (Daumen in Bild 5): Shutterstock.com/Cosmic_Design; **S. 31**: Cornelsen/Anja Poehlmann; **S. 33**: Cornelsen/Anja Poehlmann; **S. 35**: Shutterstock.com/Pasonglit Junuan; **S. 39** oben: Shutterstock.com/Funny Solution Studio, unten: Shutterstock.com/Modvector; **S. 40** oben: Shutterstock.com/ Isometrixus, unten: Shutterstock.com/spline_x; **S. 42**/A–B: Cornelsen/Anja Poehlmann; **S. 43**/C–D: Cornelsen/Anja Poehlmann; **S. 44**/A: Shutterstock.com/Le_Mon, B: Shutterstock.com/ngaga;

D: mauritius images/Steve Vidler; **S. 105**/A: Shutterstock.com/Kozyreva Elena, B: Shutterstock.com/RedKoala, C: Shutterstock.com/RedKoala, D: Shutterstock.com/Arcady, Kopf li. + re.: Cornelsen/Anja Poehlmann; **S. 106–S. 108 (Fotos)**: Cornelsen/Anja Poehlmann; **S. 108–S. 113** Emoticons: Shutterstock.com/Yefym Turkin; **S. 117** oben re.: Cornelsen/Inhouse/Mara Leibowitz, 1: Cornelsen/Grasshopper Films, 2: Cornelsen/Grasshopper Films; **S. 118** alle außer Möve: Imago Stock & People GmbH/Sylvio Dittrich; **S. 121** oben re.: Cornelsen/Anja Poehlmann, Mitte re.: Shutterstock.com/Rawpixel.com; **S. 122** oben re.: dpa Picture-Alliance/ZUMAPRESS.com/London News Pictures via ZUMA/Hugo Michiels, 1: Cornelsen/Anja Poehlmann, 2: Shutterstock.com/GCapture, 3: Shutterstock.com/MaraZe, 4: Shutterstock.com/daphnusia images; **S. 123**/A: stock.adobe.com/vm2002, B: stock.adobe.com/Ildi Papp/Ildi, US Staaten: stock.adobe.com/Racer57, Flagge: stock.adobe.com/M-KOS, Tacos: StockFood/Lawton, Becky/PhotoCuisine, Wasser: Shutterstock.com/Mariyana M; **S. 124**/A: Shutterstock.com/tanaban chuenchay, B: Shutterstock.com/Pressmaster, C: Shutterstock.com/Kimberly Shavender, D: Shutterstock.com/Botond Horvath, E: Shutterstock.com/Irina Yusupova, F: Shutterstock.com/GCapture; **S. 128** Anzug: Shutterstock.com/bybrana, Hausschuhe: Shutterstock.com/shooarts, Krawatte: Shutterstock.com/Suslik1983, Kleid: Shutterstock.com/Michael Kraus, Schuhe: Shutterstock.com/Seyfettin Karagunduz; **S. 129** oben re.: Shutterstock.com/solarseven, Mitte re.: Shutterstock.com/Digital Genetics; **S. 130**: Shutterstock.com/kibri_ho; **S. 131** oben re.: stock.adobe.com/Coprid, Mitte re.: Shutterstock.com/Bildagentur Zoonar GmbH; **S. 132**/A: Shutterstock.com/Gorodenkoff, B: Shutterstock.com/Basyn, C: Depositphotos/VOLODYMYR VAKSMAN, D: Shutterstock.com/M_Agency; **S. 133**/E: Shutterstock.com/megaflopp, F: Shutterstock.com/Roman Chazov, G: Shutterstock.com/Jacob Lund, H: stock.adobe.com/hedgehog94; **S. 134**: Cornelsen/Anja Poehlmann; **S. 135**/1: Shutterstock.com/uiliaaa, 2: Shutterstock.com/Kakigori Studio, 3: Shutterstock.com/mentalmind, 4: Shutterstock.com/BRO.vector, unten li.: Shutterstock.com/serhii.suravikin, unten re.: Shutterstock.com/Pinkcandy; **S. 136** unten re.: Shutterstock.com/Monkey Business Images; **S. 137**/A: Shutterstock.com/Simple Line, B: Shutterstock.com/samui, C: Shutterstock.com/Gigonthebeach, D: Shutterstock.com/Simple Line, E: Shutterstock.com/lineartestpilot; **S. 138**/1: Shutterstock.com/Image Source Collection, 2: stock.adobe.com/Елена Гурова, 3: Shutterstock.com/Atitaph_StockPHoTo, 4: stock.adobe.com/peopleimages.com/Katleho Seisa; **S. 140** Mädchen: Shutterstock.com/ViDI Studio. Sparschwein: Shutterstock.com/ADragan; **S. 141** oben re.: Shutterstock.com/Monkey Business Images, 1: Shutterstock.com/Konstantin Zibert, 2: Shutterstock.com/Tupungato, 3: stock.adobe.com/highwaystarz; **S. 144** alle: Cornelsen/Anja Poehlmann; **S. 145** alle: Cornelsen/Anja Poehlmann; **S. 146** alle: Cornelsen/Anja Poehlmann; **S. 147** oben re.: Cornelsen/Inhouse/Mara Leibowitz, 1 + 2: Grasshopper Films LTD; **S. 149** alle: Shutterstock.com/Tom K Photo; **S. 150**: Shutterstock.com/Franck Boston; **S. 151**/1–5: Cornelsen/Anja Poehlmann, A: stock.adobe.com/Iakov Filimonov/JackF, B: Shutterstock.com/LADO, C: Shutterstock.com/ORION PRODUCTION, D: stock.adobe.com/Production/M/M-Production, E: stock.adobe.com/Dragana Gordic; **S. 154**/1: Shutterstock.com/Daisy Daisy, 2: Shutterstock.com/Tap10, 3: Shutterstock.com/narai chal, 4: Shutterstock.com/J2R, 5: Shutterstock.com/Dragon Images, 6: Shutterstock.com/Jenny Sturm, 7: Shutterstock.com/Rawpixel.com, 8: Shutterstock.com/vichie81; **S. 155** oben re.: Cornelsen/Anja Poehlmann; **S. 157** Feuerwehr: stock.adobe.com/toa555, Ärzte: Shutterstock.com/Minerva Studio; **S. 158** oben re.: Cornelsen/Michael Fleischmann, unten re.: stock.adobe.com/Victor Moussa; **S. 159**: Shutterstock.com/Wealthylady; **S. 160** Rafting: Shutterstock.com/Aleksandr Lupin, Tauchen: Shutterstock.com/Denis Moskvinov, Brücke: stock.adobe.com/Simon Dannhauer, Rodelbahn: stock.adobe.com/Fotolia RAW, Zipline: stock.adobe.com/shiyana, Bett: Shutterstock.com/Darrin Henry, Wand: Shutterstock.com/Neirfy, Origami: Shutterstock.com/AnastasiaNi, Golf: Shutterstock.com/Jana Vackova-Vesela, Garten: Shutterstock.com/kryzhov; **S. 161** Bürstenschnitt: stock.adobe.com/schankz, gegeltes Haar: Shutterstock.com/Phovoir, Pferdeschwanz: Shutterstock.com/Prostock-studio, Ponyfrisur: Shutterstock.com/Gelpi, Zöpfe: Shutterstock.com/Nataliya Turpitko, Bart: Shutterstock.com/Roman Samborskyi, Sommersprossen: Shutterstock.com/PinkCoffee Studio, lackierte Nägel: Shutterstock.com/Subbotina Anna, Airbrush-Nägel: Shutterstock.com/Innger_Nails, Piercing: Shutterstock.com/Ludmila Ivashchenko, Tätowierung: Shutterstock.com/New Africa, Wunde: Shutterstock.com/BLACKDAY; **S. 162** Jacke: Shutterstock.com/Pixel-Shot, Kapuzenpullover: Shutterstock.com/way.uy, Pulli: Shutterstock.com/Magdalena Wielobob, Hemd: Shutterstock.com/elenovsky, Socken: Shutterstock.com/koraypolat, Turnschuhe: Shutterstock.com/Den Rozhnovsky, Sandalen: Shutterstock.com/Chiyacat, Rock: Shutterstock.com/Maffi, Strumpfhose: Shutterstock.com/Africa Studio, Damenunterwäsche: Shutterstock.com/Africa Studio, Männerunterwäsche: Shutterstock.com/Anna Chelnokova, Handschuhe: Shutterstock.com/NsdPower, Schal: Shutterstock.com/Adisa, Gürtel: Shutterstock.com/In Green, Sonnenbrille: Shutterstock.com/Jin young-in, Schmuck: Shutterstock.com/Roma Borman; **S. 164** Action Film: Shutterstock.com/FlashMovie, Karikatur: Shutterstock.com/Macrovector, Komödie: Shutterstock.com/Anneka, Kochsendung: Shutterstock.com/Supamotion, Katastrophenfilm: Shutterstock.com/Regina Erofeeva, Doku: Shutterstock.com/Wirestock Creators, Fantasiefilm: Shutterstock.com/Nejron Photo, Spielsendung: Shutterstock.com/Frame Stock Footage, Horrorfilm: Shutterstock.com/Jeff Cameron Collingwood, Reality Show: Shutterstock.com/Amy Lutz, Romanze: Shutterstock.com/chainarong06, Science-Fiction Film: Shutterstock.com/ktsdesign, Seifenoper: Shutterstock.com/oneinchpunch, Sportsendung: Shutterstock.com/Eugene Onischenko, Thriller: Shutterstock.com/DedMityay; **S. 165** alle: Shutterstock.com/Rashad Ashur; **S. 166** Rindfleisch: Shutterstock.com/MaraZe, Hähnchen: Shutterstock.com/JIANG HONGYAN, Fisch: Shutterstock.com/MaraZe, Wurst: Shutterstock.com/Einsteinstudio, Eier: Shutterstock.com/Nattika, Lamm: Shutterstock.com/TheBusinessMan; **S. 166** Schweinefleisch: Shutterstock.com/GSDesign, Erdbeere: Shutterstock.com/Tim UR, Apfel: Shutterstock.com/Roman Samokhin, Honigmelone: Shutterstock.com/Boonchuay1970, Himbeere: Shutterstock.com/Andriy Lipkan, Orange: Shutterstock.com/Valentyn Volkov, Mango: Shutterstock.com/Valentyn Volkov, Banane: Shutterstock.com/bergamont, Zitrone: Shutterstock.com/Maks Narodenko, Kirsche: Shutterstock.com/Serg64, Popcorn: Shutterstock.com/Jiri Hera, Törtchen: Shutterstock.com/Wealthylady, Muffin: Shutterstock.com/Binh Thanh Bui, Eis: Shutterstock.com/stockcreations, Donuts: Shutterstock.com/Sergey Skleznev, Gelee: Shutterstock.com/cigdem, Butter: Shutterstock.com/bigacis, Käse: Shutterstock.com/Tanya Sid, Joghurt: Shutterstock.com/pogonici, Milch: Shutterstock.com/New Africa, Sahne: Shutterstock.com/grey_and, Salat: Shutterstock.com/PotaeRin, Kartoffel: Shutterstock.com/Anna Kucherova, Tomate: Shutterstock.com/Tim UR, Aubergine: Shutterstock.com/PixaHub, Broccoli: Shutterstock.com/smspsy, Karotte: Shutterstock.com/Valentina Razumova, Kraut: Shutterstock.com/JIANG HONGYAN, Gurke: Shutterstock.com/Maks Narodenko, Knoblauch: Shutterstock.com/Maks Narodenko, Chilli: Shutterstock.com/PixaHub, Erbsen: Shutterstock.com/WIPHARAT CHAINUPAPHA, Paprika: Shutterstock.com/DronG, Zwiebeln: Shutterstock.com/Yeti studio; **S. 168** Kosmetikerin: Shutterstock.com/Rido, Call-Center-Agent: Shutterstock.com/Bojan Milinkov, Pfleger: Shutterstock.com/Pixel-Shot, Kassiererin: Shutterstock.com/hedgehog94, Zahnärztin: Shutterstock.com/Drazen Zigic, Elektronikerin: Shutterstock.com/Phovoir, Ingenieur: Shutterstock.com/Chaosamran_Studio, Anwalt: Shutterstock.com/Gorodenkoff, Rettungssanitäter: Shutterstock.com/Gorodenkoff, Klempner: Shutterstock.com/amedeoemaja, Sekretär: Shutterstock.com/DC Studio, Verkäuferin: Shutterstock.com/George Rudy, Fabrik: Shutterstock.com/Gorodenkoff, Farm: Shutterstock.com/Fotokostic, Garage: Shutterstock.com/Gorodenkoff, Labor: Shutterstock.com/Gorodenkoff; **S. 169** oben li.: Shutterstock.com/Dean Clarke, oben Mi.: Shutterstock.com/gabriel12, oben re.: stock.adobe.com/dusanpetkovic1, Mitte li.: Shutterstock.com/Monkey Business Images, Mitte Mi.: Shutterstock.com/Christian Mueller, Mitte re.: stock.adobe.com/Heliosphile, unten li.: stock.adobe.com/nowaczykfoto.pl/Mirek, unten Mi.: stock.adobe.com/Mihail, unten re.: Shutterstock.com/Bacho.

🔊 Classroom English

Good morning! *(bis 12 Uhr)*	Guten Morgen!
Good afternoon! *(nach 12 Uhr)*	Guten Tag!
Sorry, I'm late.	Entschuldigung, dass ich zu spät komme.
Can I open / close the window, please?	Kann ich bitte das Fenster öffnen / zumachen?
Can I go to the toilet, please?	Kann ich bitte zur Toilette gehen?
Goodbye. / See you tomorrow.	Auf Wiedersehen! Bis morgen.
I don't understand this exercise.	Ich verstehe die Übung nicht.
What's for homework?	Was haben wir (als Hausaufgabe) auf?
Can you help me, please?	Können Sie mir bitte helfen?
What page is it, please?	Auf welcher Seite sind wir / steht es?
What's ... in English / German?	Was heißt ... auf Englisch / Deutsch?
Can I say it in German?	Kann ich das auf Deutsch sagen?
Listen, please.	Hört bitte zu.
Open your books at page 24, please.	Schlagt bitte Seite 24 auf.
Do exercise 5 for homework, please.	Macht bitte Übung 5 als Hausaufgabe.